First Came the Family

First Came

First Came the Family

Karen M. Lindfeldt

NEW YORK   *1958*

the Family

by

Ruth M. Underhill

Illustrated by

Arminta Neal

WILLIAM MORROW AND COMPANY

CONTENTS

CHAPTER

1. WHERE DID THE FAMILY BEGIN?   9

2. WHO IS IN THE FAMILY?   22

3. THE FAMILY WAS THE WORLD   41

4. CHOOSING A MATE   59

5. WINNING A MATE   75

6. WEDDINGS   88

7. HOW MANY MATES?   109

8. MARRIED LIFE   122

9. INCREASING THE FAMILY   138

10. NAMES   156

11. CHILDHOOD   168

12. ADOLESCENCE   185

13. OLD AGE   201

BIOGRAPHICAL NOTE   211

INDEX   215

First Came the Family

CHAPTER I

Where Did the Family Begin?

IF YOU were a codfish you would not know you had ever had a mother and father or brothers and sisters. You might swim in a shoal of little wriggling silver creatures, but you would have no idea that you and they had all come out of the same batch of eggs. You would never think of helping each other, for no cod ever makes a move of that sort, no matter what the danger. Nor does any cod, however young, get care and protection from the mother who laid the eggs. In fact, after laying six million eggs, she simply swims away. If only a hundred or so baby fish grow up, the egg laying is considered successful.

Suppose that fish had the loyalty and trust in each other

which human beings develop. What a school of fish could do! They might build a barricade of seaweed, where they could hide from fishermen. Or perhaps they might foul ship rudders and even drive vessels from the sea lanes. But these actions would need more brain power than any fish possesses.

As we look through the animal kingdom, it is clear that brains are less developed in creatures which have to be self-sufficient the moment they are born. Creatures whose young are helpless, even for a little while, have time to teach them while they protect them.

Fish do not have this opportunity to learn. Each one is an individual from the moment of birth. Even the father and mother have no loyalty to each other. In fact, they are not acquainted. The female fish lays her eggs and swims away. Later a male comes to fertilize the eggs. Occasionally a female fish seeks out a safe place for her eggs—shallow water or a pool hidden under branches. Here there is a slight hint of maternal care. In some species this care is one of the female's most urgent instincts. Family life is completely absent from the fish world, although no fish eats the eggs of its own kind.

Without care for the young and without the loyalty that grows from it, there might never have been a family, a tribe, or a nation. Yet we can search through millions of years of animal life without finding more than the briefest beginnings of a real family. Often during the great cumbersome process of evolution animals started to produce a family group, but each time this development was sidetracked.

Some of these starts took place among the fishes, but the young were cared for by the father, not the mother. Instinct tells the male stickleback, a little spiny fresh-water fish, to hollow out a nest near the side of a stream and to invite a female in. She comes, lays about a thousand eggs, and swims away. The father guards the eggs and lets fresh water into the nest now and then to keep it whole-some. After the eggs hatch, he guards the small fry from danger for at least a month.

Another example is the male seahorse. On his front he has a pouch where he carries his mate's eggs until they hatch. He has a small family, not the hundreds, thousands, or millions of young which most fish produce. But fish did not develop family structure any further than this. Their chance of surviving as a group depends simply on their being so numerous that all cannot be killed off. But if there is to be a real family, care and loyalty are necessary.

There is a little more care of the young among reptiles than among fishes, perhaps because they have fewer young. Most reptile mothers bury their eggs in the sand before leaving them, and the little skink lizard curls her-self around her eggs and turns them over in the sun until they hatch. Some reptile fathers also take charge of the hatching. The male Surinam toad, for instance, carries his mate's eggs on his back. But in any case, hatching is the end of family life. The young are able to take care of them-selves when they come out of the eggs, and the father or mother leaves them immediately.

Many insects do not live after they have mated and laid their eggs. The mother does use some care in choosing the place for the eggs, but usually family life does not go beyond this stage. The mason wasp, however, does a little more. She digs a hole for her one egg and also provides it with food by stinging some flies into unconsciousness and putting them in the hole. When the egg hatches, the young one will have live food. This young one is not a wasp; it is a wormlike larva. It has a very strange period of infancy, which substitutes for the lack of a mother's care. Instinct tells the wingless larva to make a cocoon, and out of that it comes as an adult insect, ready to take care of itself.

Ants and bees appear to show some signs of family life. Adult ants work together like armies or factory gangs. In Africa a swarm of these tiny creatures, each a half inch long, can build an anthill higher than a house. These ants are a family, for they are all hatched from eggs laid by one female. The wormlike infants are nursed and fed by older sisters, and finally they develop into workers or soldiers who stay to take care of the home and the new broods. If they become princes or princesses, they fly away to start a new anthill. Worker or sister bees also tend infant larvae, and sometimes they give them better food than they have ever had themselves. They fly off to find nectar and bring it all back to the hive. Unlike a fish, which finds food only for itself, a bee never acts as an individual, flying off to enjoy her nectar alone.

Thus on the surface bees and ants seem to form ideally united and self-sacrificing families. But bees and ants have no choice. They have a built-in system of instincts, which drives them to do certain things and no others. No bee or ant ever has the desire to go off alone, and if she did she

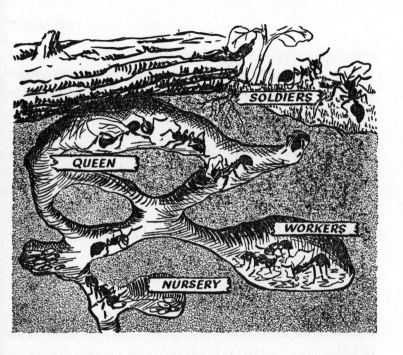

would die. She is not an individual but a part of a whole, like a blood vessel in a body. The bees in a hive are more like a set of robots than like a family.

Birds, however, do have some family life, and there is good reason for this. For one thing, birds have small families. When they became air-borne creatures, they left behind them the four-legged enemies which used to pursue them. A female bird did not need to lay a hundred or even a dozen eggs to be sure that a few of the young would live. Six eggs or less were plenty, and it was possible that all of the nestlings would reach maturity.

A small number of children is the essence of real family life. Parents can then recognize and take care of the children, as fish can never do. Bird eggs are also different from fish eggs, for they cannot be left alone to hatch. They must be kept warm, or the little developing creatures inside the eggs will die. It usually takes the care of two parents to handle this job. The mother must sit on the eggs, and the father must bring her food. Even among birds, however, this family system is not always followed. For example, the young of the phalarope of Africa and the emu, a kind of little ostrich, are cared for by the father.

"Catch him while he hatch eggs," I was told by a native. "Deep in bush find pile of twigs. He little black neck sticking out."

"Where is the female?"

He waved his hand. "Oh, she go off. Find more man."

I didn't believe it until I went home and looked up information on these birds. Nature has often tried this system of father care, but so far it has not been successful enough to become general.

Many birds, and especially the songbirds, seem to have a model family life. Courting, choosing a nesting place, producing young, and caring for them take up at least half of a songbird's year; and these are all family matters. The rest of the year (if they don't have another family) is a resting period. Then they fly to a warmer climate and gather strength for a new family venture, usually with a different mate.

The time from egg laying to the departure of the young birds may last anywhere from a few weeks to several months, and it is a time of devoted parent care. The young birds, naked and helpless, are real babies, dependent on their parents. A bird mother recognizes her own children, as a codfish never could. The children not only recognize her, they depend on her. This dependence is the very foundation of family life.

The mother waits on the baby just as assiduously as a human mother. Usually the job demands the father, too. Two blue titmice, bringing worms and insects to their young, made 475 trips to the nest in 17 hours. The mother also cleans the nest, and she keeps marauders away by fluttering over it or leading them astray.

When it is time for the young bird to fly, it goes through a real period of training. Anyone who has a robin's nest near his house can see the parent birds fluttering and calling like the most progressive of teachers. Sometimes they even use discipline. I remember a fat young robin, three days out of the nest, which sat helplessly on the ground, cheeping for its mother to bring food. She brought three worms and then, with a squawk, she flew away. It was time for that adolescent to get worms for himself.

If it took a bird three or four years to grow up, it is possible a real family would develop. Bird fathers and mothers might have some time, after the babies were able to feed themselves, to become really acquainted with them. The brothers, sisters, and cousins might develop feelings of loyalty, and perhaps form a clan or tribe. But bird life is too short for that step toward a real family. It is even too short for eagles, which stay together longer than the little songbirds.

In the few weeks of infancy, the bird does get used to having others of his kind around him, just as the human baby does. As the parents bring him food and teach him to fly, he begins to trust them. But as soon as he is able to get food for himself, the parents fly away and leave him. They leave each other, too. There is no time for the young to learn to help the old and to help each other. Birds have only one part of family life—parent care. Yet that care counts for something. When it is time to migrate in the fall, a young bird seeks out others of his kind, and they wait together until a big flock has gathered. Are they perhaps brothers, sisters, and cousins, whose parents all nested in the same area? We do not know if they recognize their kin, perhaps by a special song accent, but we do know they recognize birds of their own kind and trust them enough to fly thousands of miles with them.

Mammals, our own biological order, have bigger bodies, bigger brains, and longer infancy than any of these other creatures do. The mammal mother gives suck to her young out of her own body, and this act makes for a more intimate relationship than a bird's warming of unhatched eggs does. The gap between birth and instinctive behavior, which must be filled with teaching, is much wider among mammals than among birds. In fact, teaching can really change the young animal's behavior. Reports tell of kittens who have been brought up with rats and never hurt them. The mammal mother seems to love her babies, as anyone who has seen a cat with her kittens or a cow with her calf can testify. The young grow up in real contact with their parents and build up an association that will last through life.

Most mammals, however, know only one parent, and that is the mother. Mammals, like birds, have a season when all their bodily functions are prepared for mating. When that time comes, the male cannot help seeking a mate, and when it passes, most males want nothing to do with the mate or the children. So the male cat, dog, moose, buffalo, or the bull mates vigorously when nature bids him and the female is ready. When the mating is over, he moves off alone.

Of course there are exceptions. Lions have to range far and use a great deal of energy to get their prey, so the male waits on the female while she suckles her young and cannot hunt. He may even stay around long enough to teach his cubs the difficult art of hunting. The male wolf also stays with his family for the same reason. But the female dog or cat, deer or buffalo, can easily get food for her young or teach them to graze, and so her mate does not stay with her. Most mammal families, tender and loving as they may seem, are one-sided, and they can never develop a clan or a tribe.

The wolf pack and the buffalo or deer herd are a partial start toward clans or tribes, but these are not permanent arrangements. The animals gather at some times of the year for the sake of getting food more conveniently. Yet perhaps these groups are like migrating flocks of birds— collections of animals which have learned to trust each other. Old Plains hunters tell of the remarkable organization of a buffalo herd. The females and calves stay in the middle, and the bulls are on the outside to protect them.

Animals which have become friends of man, such as the dog, horse, camel, sheep, yak, and elephant, are all herd animals in their wild state. If they were solitary fighters,

like spiders, they would not trust their own kind, and perhaps they would never have trusted man.

Apes, man's distant cousins, have a very important
physical trait in common with man. Their females do not
have one specific courting season during a year, so males
and females do not lose interest in each other after mating
and go off in separate groups, as birds and other animals
do. Ape mates often stay together for years, and they show
the beginnings of a true family.Gibbons, chimpanzees, and
gorillas travel in family groups of parents and children,
and the father is the head of the group. The children get
considerable training in how to find food and avoid
enemies, and they do more than merely accept help and
food until they are able to leave home. They actually help
the family by calling to them when they find good fruit and
by giving warning of enemies. However, these groups are
still not like the family groups of modern America, for
instance. Except for the gibbons, the father may have
several wives, and they live together as peaceably as harem
wives. The mothers seem to share in the care of the children, just as human mothers do in some countries where
men have several wives.

Human families have formed in many different ways,
depending on the particular time and country concerned.
As there are reasons for animal behavior, so there are
reasons for human ways. People at any given time usually
follow the grouping that is most useful for them. Sometimes a hundred relatives cling together like ants, although
their grouping is controlled by reasoning instead of by

instinct. Sometimes the only true unit consists of a father, a mother, and a few children.

All normal human beings, however, live in families for at least part of their lives. The children have a far longer period of companionship with their father and mother, and perhaps their brothers and sisters, than birds or animals do. Even the few who do not have families accept this grouping as natural and right. The average human being, after ten, fifteen, or twenty years in some sort of family, has an urge to belong to even larger groups. He is a herd animal, not for part of the year like the buffalo, but all the time. Because of this urge, human beings have developed clans, tribes, and nations. Family life teaches that urge, and without a family, or some substitute for it, no human being could ever be prepared to live with others.

CHAPTER 2

Who Is in the Family?

LOOK DOWN the street of a modern real-estate development. The houses, in their green, yellow, and pink paint,
are as fresh and pretty as flowers. But they are small!
They are meant for the average American family—father,
mother, and children. In recent years the statistical average number of children per family in this country was two
and a half, but now it has gone up to three.

This tight little group is the *core* family. It is the very
seed and beginning of family life. From it relatives of
several generations branch out: grandparents, uncles,
aunts, cousins of all degrees. Today few of these kinsfolk
live with parents and children in the new little houses.

They may be in some other part of town, or perhaps in a different town altogether. Young children often grow up without even knowing the names of their distant cousins.

Now take a drive through the old farming country of New England, where many of the houses were built over a hundred years ago. The big white buildings, circled by elm trees, look as large as some European palaces. Yet they were not built to house an army of servants, as the palaces were. They were filled by the family, and often the family was so large that no hired help was needed. There were more children in those days; and one or more grandparents, a maiden aunt or two, a widowed aunt with her children, a bachelor uncle, and perhaps an orphan cousin or an adopted child might live in the house too.

Taking in those relatives was not a matter of charity, for they could all be useful. A small child could pull weeds and run errands, a grandfather could sharpen saws and mend harness, while a grandmother could darn socks and take care of cuts and bruises. And the family could hardly get along without the more able-bodied relatives. But try to transfer such a working group to one of the new little houses, crammed with work-saving gadgets! The able-bodied relatives would only be in the way. Moreover, it is easier to get work outside the family now, and many people prefer to have jobs and to rent rooms of their own, instead of staying in the family home. Grandparents can, perhaps, be baby sitters, but renting a house large enough to make them comfortable is very expensive.

Many modern families must also be movable. Their property is usually not in the form of an ancestral farm but in money or securities which can be taken anywhere. Some day the father may get a new job in another city, and the family may have to move. It would be hard and expensive to take the old people along. So the core family often prefers a small house it can maintain by itself. There are reasons for the small family today, just as there were reasons once for the huge families.

As we look over the world's families, at various times and in different places, we can see that there is usually a reason for each type of family in the lifeway of the people. One statement, however, is always true: every family begins with a core family. Relatives may cluster around it, or there may be extra wives. Sometimes the uncles, aunts, or cousins have special duties which modern people could never imagine. But there is always the basic core. Beginning with the earliest families, we can trace the development of family organization from the core family to the larger groupings and back to the core family again. We shall see that a close connection exists between the changes in family structure and the needs of the family members.

Unfortunately, we know far less about the lives of early men than about those of the fish and the reptiles which lived at the same time. Since fish and reptiles are guided by instinct, they live today just about as they did a million years ago. Men, with their more developed brains and their working hands, have changed so much and so dramatically that we have to dig, study, and guess in order to have any picture of our own ancestors. We have uncovered stone tools, the ashes of age-old campfires, and the bones of animals that were eaten. And by studying how primitive people in out-of-the-way corners of the world live to-day, we are able to learn a great deal about the habits of early man, for he used much the same methods of hunting and food gathering.

Primitive people today live in small groups, since large ones would scare the animals they hunt and would use up the food plants. Their family groups are core families. From this we guess that early men lived in core families by the time they could make stone tools and fire. Probably they were much like the Eskimos, the Paiute Indians, and the Andaman Islanders of the Pacific today.

These families differ from those of all other mammals, even apes, because even little children contribute mature help. Sitting around a Paiute camp, I have watched a little boy of three bringing small sticks for the fire. A girl of five was helping a toddler to walk. This co-operation does not happen in any other mammal family. Young chimpanzees and gorillas at that stage are grown animals, able to forage for themselves. If they did not leave the family voluntarily, they would soon be driven away, lest they made love to the father or mother.

The human child has at least twelve years of depend-ence on others. During those years he learns to trust and work with his kind in a way that no bird or mammal does. The human child learns gradually with the help of speech, and he becomes prepared for co-operation in any situation he may meet. These habit-forming years of trust and affection are the very basis of communal living. Mankind might never have joined together in tribes or towns with-out them. A child who is brought up without trust and affection is sometimes unable to co-operate, and he may become one of society's enemies. Among the Paiute Indians and other groups which have simple core families today, there seems to be plenty of affection.

Families of primitive people join together today, just as they did in ancient times. A family may manage by itself during the winter, when it lives on dried stores, but at other times help is needed. Perhaps it wants to put up a hut or organize a game hunt. The father looks for someone he can trust with this project, and who should that be but his own brother or sister? They were brought up in the same hut with him, and he knows them through and through. Their ways may be bad, but at least his own relatives are safer than strangers.

So, in addition to the organization of the individual core family, there is this larger grouping which consists of the core families of brothers and sisters, living and camping together. The men help each other in hunting. The women go out in a group, with babies on their backs, to gather wild plants. If one young mother is busy at home, another will pick up her crying baby and even nurse it. A child grows up safe and wanted among all these kinsfolk. As one old Indian said to me, "My relatives are the hair on my legs, the other end of my navel cord."

There is only one thing the family cannot give a young man, and that is a wife. If he were an ape, he could make love to one of his sisters, but from earliest times human beings have felt that any love-making within the core family is a sin. So the boy must look elsewhere for a mate. However, he cannot start courting any female he may meet, the way a bird does. He and his bride will live with his family or hers for many years, and both families want something to say about the match.

Getting himself a mate will be a matter of much negotiation between his camp and a nearby camp which is not too strange to his people. Perhaps he will go to the other camp to live; perhaps he will bring his bride home. It isn't very important where they live, since the family doesn't own land and has few goods to carry around. The important thing is that now the family has a whole group of allies. As more and more young people marry, the number of allies will increase, until the whole neighborhood is full of friends, instead of strangers. This may be the fundamental reason for the beginning of the custom of exogamy —marriage outside the family group.

Exogamy produces a broader family structure, for the camp of core families of brothers and sisters is now related by marriage to the camps of other families. If exogamy goes on long enough, everyone in the neighborhood may come to be related—some of them many times over.

I came across something like this when I first went to study the Papago Indians in southern Arizona. I made friends with a sprightly old grandmother, who adopted me as her younger sister. In fact, I could hardly have been received among the Indians if I had not belonged to some family, for a stranger would have had no rights. The old lady and I drove about the reservation in my car, which she loved. Whenever we arrived at a new village, we would draw up in the central square, and crowds of men would appear to stare at us. As was proper, the women kept out of the way. My ancient sister would look over the crowd, then call to some young man, "Grandson, have you a cigarette?" One was always forthcoming.

Finally I chided her. "Look here, Elder Sister, these young men you speak to can't all be your grandsons! I believe you just pick out one who looks as if he had some tobacco and call him that."

She was offended. "No, Younger Sister. Of course they are my grandsons." When I looked incredulous, she went on. "You know, from my brothers and sisters, near and far."

Then I understood. These young men included the grandsons of her own brothers and sisters and those of all her cousins on both sides. She told me that they were my grandsons, too, because I was her sister, and instructed me to treat them better.

"But Elder Sister!" I protested. "I'll bet there are fifty of them. Do you treat them all alike?"

She shook her head at my stupidity, as she often had to do, and assured me that she knew the difference between the near ones and the far ones. "I treat the near ones better, and they do the same to me. But if I were in trouble and no near ones were around, I could go to a far one. At least he wouldn't be a stranger."

That incident is a good example of how primitive people lump relatives together. But obviously if my "elder sister's" generous way of counting relatives were fully carried out, the whole country would be simply a network of kinsfolk. How can a mate be found if everyone is related? People all over the world have recognized this problem. They have distinguished between relatives who are close, whom they do not marry, and those who are more distant. To us the problem seems very simple. Relatives on both sides of the family, up to one's first cousins, are generally regarded as too closely related for marriage. We base this position on biological and religious grounds. Primitive people knew nothing about biology, but they believed that gods and spirits forbade marrying within the core family.

The defining of relationships beyond the core family varies, but the usual arrangement is to divide a family straight down the middle, separating the relatives on the father's side from those on the mother's. This brings us to a development in family organization beyond that of the

groups of core families. When we talk about the Rocke-
fellers or the Roosevelts, we have in mind a line of descent
that can be traced through several generations. This is
known as lineage, or the *stem* family, and it is a more permanent group than the little core families, which may
separate from each other at any time. The stem family can
hold land and titles through generations, as many have,
and it can perpetuate a name.

In tracing a line of descent, which side of the family
shall be featured? To us there seems only one answer—the
father's. The Zulus of South Africa share our view. Ask a
Zulu who his relatives are, and he will enumerate the members of his father's family. He calls his mother's side of the
family People of the Tribes, and no matter how close they
are to him, they do not owe him duties as his father's people
do. The father acts as family priest. He is also the absolute
owner of everyone and everything in the kraal—the village
or social unit—and has the right to thrash, bind, starve,
imprison, or mutilate any member of the family. According to reports, however, most Zulu fathers are usually
kindly patriarchs rather than stern rulers.

This family pattern is called father descent, or the
patrilineal system, and it is a well-known pattern in every
country in the world, including our own. True, we regard
our mother's people as our relatives. But like the Zulus and
many other peoples—the hunting and fighting Indians of
North and South America, the herders of Siberia, and the
Arabs of the desert, for example—we take our father's name
and count our ancestry back through him, his father, and
all the fathers before that.

The father passes his name and wealth on to his son who, when he marries, passes the name and wealth on to <u>his</u> son.

When the daughter marries, she takes her husband's name, and her children trace their ancestry through their father.

FATHER (PATRILINEAL) DESCENT shown by black arrows in shaded area

However, there are people who trace their ancestry through their mothers and not through their fathers. The famous Iroquois Indians of New York counted descent through their mothers. At the head of each long house—the communal dwelling of the Iroquois—was an old woman, who ruled over her daughters, their husbands, and their children. When her son married, he went to live in his wife's long house, where he was ruled over by another matriarch. This pattern of family life is called mother descent, or the matrilineal system. It has been used by important tribes in all parts of the world.

Elaborate theories have been advanced to account for the matrilineal and patrilineal systems. The more important parent, however, generally seems to have been the one who was the main provider for the family. The Zulus were cattle people, and cattle belonged to the men. The Iroquois were farmers, and their huge fields were worked by the women, while the men were off trading and fighting. This division of labor and the customs that went with it developed long ago, when early groups began to settle down. Before that time, however, people had to move about to get their living, and both men and women did their share of providing food. Men went off on hunting trips to get meat; women stayed at home with the children. Having almost no housework or mending to do, they went out with their babies on their backs to dig roots and pick berries. In time the men learned to tame animals for use instead of killing them, and the women began to plant a few seeds around the hut. Thus in many places farming came to be women's work, while herding belonged to men.

Most families did some of both, but one source of food or the other became more important, depending on where they lived. If a family settled in open-pasture country, the men took care of the herds, and often the women could not plant at all. Their family organization usually became patrilocal (families living at the husband's home) and patrilineal. But just the opposite happened when a group found itself in a fertile valley where there were plenty of wild plants, but hunting meant long journeys. Then the woman taught plant care to her daughter, who eventually would inherit her mother's fields. This family became organized along matrilineal lines.

In a group that is matrilineal and matrilocal (families living at the wife's home), the husband is more or less a visitor. Trobriand Islanders in the South Pacific call him stranger. Among the Zuñi Indians, farming villagers of Arizona, the husband does not bring his important ceremonial possessions to his wife's house until he is a middle-aged man with several children. By that time he can feel the place is really his home.

But even in these matrilineal families, women are never the rulers except in the house. The men are still more important, since they are occupied with fighting and government; and the family authority in these larger matters is the woman's brother, a member of the core family of her childhood. He also disciplines the children and looks after the ceremonial life of the family. The woman's husband has little authority, since he has come to the family from a different home. This may sound like a humiliating situation for the husband, but we must remember that he has all

The daughter inherits her mother's name, clan, and wealth, and then passes them on to _her_ daughter.

MOTHER (MATRILINEAL) DESCENT shown by black arrows in shaded area

When the son marries, his children trace their ancestry through their mother.

these rights in his sister's home. To his own children he is a friend, a teacher, and, apparently, a loved one.

The same general arrangement exists among many farming Indians, such as the Hopi, the Navaho, and the Iroquois, and even among some Plains hunters and some fishermen of the Northwest coast. It works well in parts of the South Pacific and South America. Across Africa there is a belt of farming people where the young husband lives with his wife's parents until he has several children. Then he may set up a house of his own. It is possible, too, for a matrilineal group to be patrilocal when it is more convenient.

There are still matrilineal families in parts of the world, but they are passing. We can see the reason for this. In general, men have become the main providers, for they have taken over one function after another once carried on by women. The plow, drawn by an ox or a horse, requires a man driver, and when it came into use it supplanted the woman's hoe in many places. The potter's wheel enabled men to produce pottery in large quantities, with the result that women's handmade jars were no longer an important contribution to the family income. This development also happened in weaving and other arts, even doctoring. It is interesting to speculate on what will happen now that women have come back into the picture as providers.

The distinction between the patrilineal (father descent) and matrilineal (mother descent) family organizations may sound clear-cut, but of course there are many variations. Occasionally, families are a mixture of the two.

In fact, in all areas of human behavior there are always so many shadings that it is often misleading to make any flat statements. Circumstances and people are so different, and they keep changing so much, that all descriptions must be full of the words *usually* and *not often*, instead of *always* and *never*.

So far this chapter has dealt with core families, stem families, and their combinations. Yet there is a further development, which at one time was the most important family grouping of all. This is the gathering of the stem families into clans. The Zulus, the Iroquois, and the Crow are all organized in this way. Most of us have heard of the Scottish clans, with their distinctive tartans and their wild fights with each other. These clans, headed by chiefs to whom all members were related in the male line, were only a remnant of the clans which used to exist throughout the British Isles and in Europe, including ancient Greece and Rome. There were also clans in Asia, Africa, and the Americas.

In essence, the clan is a group of people who trace their descent from the same ancestor, either in the male or the female line. So far this definition might apply to a stem family, but the stem family's ancestor is a known, real person, who lived not too far back in time. The clan's ancestor may be a god or a mythical hero, who lived so long ago that relationships with him cannot really be reckoned. Nevertheless, all clan members regard themselves as brothers and sisters and cannot marry each other.

Usually the clan has a chief; he may be the oldest male in the direct line of descent. The clan may own land, as the

Chinese clans did, or sacred objects, as the Fox Indians of Indiana did. It has a name, like the Snipe and the Beaver Clans of the Iroquois, or the Little Water Clan of the Navaho. Sometimes the name refers to an animal believed to have helped the ancestor of the clan, or perhaps to have actually been the ancestor. Often a clan will not eat the animal whose name it has chosen. The clan may have a right to special functions; for example, the chief of certain Hopi towns in our Southwest must be of the Bear Clan.

In the Americas we sometimes find a whole tribe divided into halves, with a number of clans in each. The Omaha Indians called their halves Sky People and Earth People; the Creeks named theirs Red and White. Usually these halves practiced exogamy, so that a person born in one half had to marry a member of the other. Sometimes several clans grouped together. In the Old World clans rarely reached this stage, but they often grew to immense sizes. One in ancient India contained 10,000 people. In China, everyone bearing the same surname belonged to one clan. There were only a few clans in the whole country, and they became so powerful that at one time the imperial government used the heads of the clans as their officials. In Europe the clans once were fighting units. With their deep loyalties and their tight organization, they often functioned as states in the days before states existed. Other fighting units existed in Scotland and the Balkans, and in our Kentucky mountains a similar pattern of fighting-and-feuding clans developed.

Clans had their strongest and longest life in places where there was a weak government or none at all. In the history of every nation it took a long time for men to act together on the basis of patriotism or loyalty to a lord. Loyalty to clan brothers and the clan leader often preceded that stage and paved the way for it. And, of course, before the clan came the family. The allocating of specific duties and rights to each person in the family was a way of organizing a little society for the protection of all its members. There was a very long period in history when this kind of organization was the only one. In fact, each family was its own world.

CHAPTER 3

The Family Was the World

A MODERN American boy wants to go to college. Perhaps his parents can pay all of his expenses, but often that is impossible. The boy may apply for a scholarship, given by people he will never meet, or he may earn the money to pay for his education by working for strangers. Often he goes to a college that is located far from home, where he makes a place for himself among total strangers. When he gives gifts at Christmas, some will go to the home people, but others will be given to those new classmates rather than to any distant relations. If he gets into trouble at school, it is the college dean who will deal with him, and his parents may never hear of it.

Yet there are parts of the world where such independence is unimaginable. It was also once unimaginable among our own ancestors. A college, a business concern, a nation, where strangers can work together without fear, is the result of a very long development. In the history of every group of people there was a time when all strangers were enemies. Whatever needed to be done in the way of education, discipline, help, or amusement was done by a person's family. In fact, the family was the world.

Once I heard a young employee of a government bureau trying to persuade a bright Indian boy to leave home so that he could train himself for a job.

"My family wouldn't like it," said the boy.

The white man brushed that aside. "What does that matter? You're an individual. You should do what's best for *yourself*."

This might be perfectly good advice for a boy of the white man's own group. But for the Indian boy, leaving his huge family of parents, uncles, and cousins would be like going to the moon. His tribe was still at the stage where no one could be trusted and relied upon outside the protecting army of relatives.

Most primitive people scarcely knew anyone outside this group. Among wandering, food-gathering folk, where only a few families camped together, this might mean very limited contacts indeed, until the yearly feast or hunt when one had a chance to look at unknown allies, and perhaps even speak to them. On these occasions boys and girls eyed each other, and families were asked to make proposals of marriage. As groups grew larger and settled down, there

DISCIPLINE

EDUCATION

RELIGION

THE
FAMILY
WAS
THE
WORLD

might be whole villages composed only of kinsfolk. This meant that all one's playmates and friends were relatives. The girl had two sets of friends—one for her girlhood and one for her married life. To us this seems a very restricted circle, but it meant great practice in getting along with others.

The Lovedu, a Negro group in Africa, live in villages of father-descent relatives. Visitors who come to these villages are impressed by the happy chatter of the people as they go about their communal activities—groups of women pounding grain together, groups of girls going off for firewood, children playing around the hut of one woman or another. They are all relatives, and they have learned from childhood to have their good times in each other's society.

Dr. Margaret Mead was intimate for some months with a group of girls in Samoa. One was unattractive and unfriendly, the kind of child who might have been left out of the play in a modern school. When Dr. Mead inquired whether the children liked her, the answer was, "Of course. She's a relative."

A Papago Indian once told me how the men of his village worked together to build a new house. They first had to go long distances to get wood for the poles, as well as the stems of cactus to weave through them. Then they had to dig a foundation, set the poles in the ground, put up the walls and the roof, and cover the roof with heavy earth, all of which meant backbreaking work for several days. During that time the host fed the whole group.

"Did everybody work all day?" I asked.

"Well, no," he answered. "Some were kind of lazy. And I guess some didn't work at all."

"I suppose they weren't invited to eat then."

The Indian was amazed at my remark. "Of course I fed them. They were relatives."

At every feast and gathering in most primitive groups, all relatives were included as a matter of course. A person might be shy, sullen, selfish, or greedy, but he never had to fear being left out. His whole social life was provided for. This was brought out very clearly when I talked to a young Indian who had gone to a city for the first time to get a job. He returned after three months, and I asked him if he had been able to find work. He told me that he had been working but had left the city because the people didn't like him. I had visions of some ugly race prejudice and asked carefully, "What did they do?"

"They didn't talk to me," he answered.

"Did you talk to *them?*"

He stared at me. It had never occurred to him that he could change their attitude by anything he said. At home his social life was completely laid out for him, and there was nothing he could say or do to change it.

A primitive group such as his provided for very specific ways of behaving toward each member. Every child had to learn which kind of cousin was which and how he was supposed to treat each of them. In some families he had to learn which aunts and uncles were older than his parents and which were younger, and behave very differently toward each age group. Moreover, different terms were used in addressing relatives, depending on whether the speaker was male or female.

Rules like these must have developed through the long periods during which human beings had to live in close groups, both for mutual help and for protection. Most primitive people still live in such groups, unless their livelihood makes them wanderers. But even among wandering tribes, there is usually a gathering of families for part of the year. The home may be a village, as with the farming people in Africa, Melanesia, or our Southwest. It may be a collection of tents or huts, as with the Siberian herders or our Plains hunters. It may be a huge communal house, as with the people of tropical South America or the Pacific coast fishermen. In any case, the duties and privileges of family members are pretty well prescribed, and each person knows how he should behave toward all the others in his group.

I realized how intricate these relationships can be when I went to a rodeo with a Crow Indian friend of mine. I recognized her brother, who was standing nearby, and suggested that she invite him over to sit on the fence with us. She did not ask him to join us, so I called the young man and he came. He did not sit beside his sister, nor did he speak to her. Later I learned that a sister, whom a Crow cannot marry, is treated with as much respect as any strange lady would be. He sat beside me because, being white, I did not count. Soon an Indian girl of his sister's age passed by, and he called her over in a very familiar way. When she came, he jokingly pulled her up onto the fence, then tried to push her off. I turned to his sister in perplexity. "Why is he so friendly with her when he doesn't even talk to you?"

Words failed the sister, but I discovered the explanation later. The second girl was the young man's cross-cousin—the child of his father's sister. Among his people such cousins were not considered direct relations; instead, they were treated as particularly close and intimate friends. All his life the Crow would have the right to treat this young woman almost as familiarly as he could a wife, but he would never be able to treat his sister this way.

In many tribes a brother and sister behave more distantly than a strange young man and a strange young lady would today. Girls and boys of Plains Indian families began wearing clothes at about the age of seven. After that

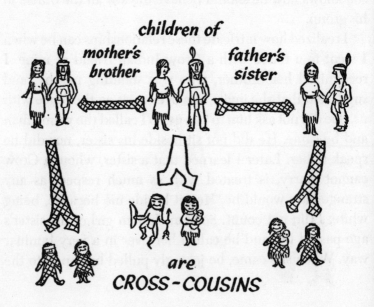

children of
mother's brother
father's sister
are
CROSS-COUSINS

they never touched each other, even to hand something to each other, and they never stayed in a tepee alone together. If a brother entered the tent and found only his sister there, he left immediately. Yet all their lives they were expected to make each other fine gifts. She gave him leatherwork, and he gave her meat and horses. I remember a festivity at an Indian school where an old man won a potato race. When he received a prize of dried fruit he carried it to an old woman—his sister. "How thoughtful," said the white people, not realizing that he was obeying an ancient rule. In Melanesia, too, a brother and sister make their richest gifts to each other, all the while maintaining a respectful distance. Sometimes all the parallel cousins—children of the father's brother or the mother's sister—get the same privileged treatment.

children of
father's brother   **mother's sister**

are
PARALLEL COUSINS

Naturally there are flare-ups among relatives at times, but many primitive family systems successfully avoid most of them by allocating specific emotional roles to their various members. A Crow Indian may be rebuked and advised by the sons of members of his father's clan. From them he must take a scolding or a teasing meekly, even in public, while if another sort of relative did the same thing, there would be a family quarrel. Many people all over the world set aside certain relatives with whom one may joke, even insultingly. Generally these joking relatives are the ones to whom the child owes no direct obedience. The custom grew up without any important psychological release being intended, but it has proved most useful. There are times when every person feels the need to let off steam, and the victim of the outburst is usually an intimate friend or, even worse, a wife or a husband. Sometimes the victim does not take it well, and bad feelings result. We might envy the American Indian groups, the Australians, and the Pacific Islanders, whose joking relatives must take insult and bad language with a smile. Sometimes the relative is permitted to reciprocate, but most often he must find someone whom *he* is entitled to insult.

There are certain relatives one never treats in this way. When I asked my Crow friend if he joked with his mother's family, he was shocked. "Sure not. Treat fine. Never talk bad."

"And what do they do for *you?*" I asked.

"Give things. Help. Like mother."

In our study of preliterate groups, we get a picture of a fairly complete little society. There are people one respects, people one helps, people to play with, people to joke with. All of these relationships exist in the modern world, but we can choose the people with whom we have them, and we can change our relationships with them if we wish to. In the primitive's world they are settled for him and cannot be changed except under special circumstances, usually involving a ceremony. This arrangement makes for calmness, a quality that many primitive people have. It is rudely shattered when, like my Indian boy, they have to make a world for themselves among strangers.

The primitive family also took care of the education of its members, as I shall discuss in more detail later. The teaching of children by strangers is a comparatively late development in any people's history. Education was usually handled by the core family, the close relatives, or the clan. Thus it was certain that a child would grow up with the very same ideas and habits that were believed and practiced by all the members of his little world. Family education was an effective way of ensuring that all the citizens of that world would act together and even feel together. It is no wonder that people coming from such family worlds today are aghast at the variety of behavior and opinions they find in a modern city. I remember a brilliant young Navaho Indian who was given a scholarship to one of our universities. I asked him how he liked the course in philosophy, and he shook his head. "The professor told us that some people think this way, and some think that way. But he never told us what was *right*."

As the family met the needs for social life and for education, so it had its own arrangements for maintaining

law and order. The chief commandment was: anything
that injures the family is wrong. Therefore, no one within
the family could steal from another or do violence to him,
for that would cause bad feeling within the family. Nor did
they permit anything that would injure the family reputation. Elders were continually adjuring the young, "If
you behave like that, our family will get a bad name. We
shall not be respected." A lazy person who did not help
with the family work was not denied his share of food or
his place at feasts, but he was told, "You give us a bad
name."

To moderns, this would not be very effective. In fact, it
is not meaningful today to young Indians who are making
their way in the cities. Inevitably the complete family
world must break down for them when they have to live
under laws made for strangers. But where the family was
the world, shame was a strong motive. Even in our society
a child at school or a member of a club would be very
unhappy if all the people in his group looked down on him,
and he might make an effort to become more acceptable.
In the same way, the family member could generally be
shamed into doing more or less what was expected of him.

Sometimes more drastic punishment was needed. A
clan head among the Creek Indians of Georgia used to
scratch lazy or misbehaving boys with the sharp-toothed
jaw of a garfish. Often there were physical punishments
for unfaithful wives. Sometimes adult men who were constant disturbers of the peace or who disgraced the group
in a serious way—perhaps by practicing sorcery or committing murder—had to be dealt with. Such people were

not punished physically, because the family and the tribe to which it belonged were very reluctant to do harm to one of their members. But they pronounced a sentence which was almost as bad as death—banishment.

This punishment was not inflicted unless all the family agreed. There was generally a meeting of the elders and a serious discussion as to whether the member could be shamed into reforming. If he seemed hopeless he was officially put out of the family. No member would give him food, shelter, or help. If his own people took this attitude, everyone else would too, since an individual had no standing except as a member of a family. The sentence was like exile as practiced later by nations. In fact, it was the forerunner of such treatment, since the family was actually a little nation. The exile might sneak around, trying to hunt or steal food, but now that he was regarded as a stranger, and therefore an enemy, he was likely to be killed on sight by anybody. Only in modern days, when a person exiled in this way can escape to a different country, has such a punishment ceased to be so dreadful.

It was still a powerful force in China fifty years ago. A person who visited there at that time tells of a young man who had offended his family by having an illicit affair with a young married sister-in-law while her husband was away. There were government agencies to which the family could have protested, but it feared disgrace. So the men of the family, in solemn council, disowned their relative and informed their clan. This meant that the youth could not find a position in China, for it was impossible to get one without the influence of the clan. Unless he could somehow earn money to emigrate, his life would be ruined.

Matters were different when the offense was against another family. The offender's family might rebuke him in private and might even outlaw him, but in public it would stand by him to a man against the other family. The whole family or clan would fight and risk death, not for the individual but for the honor of the group. The offended clan would behave in very much the same way that a modern nation does. After an incident, the offended nation asks for apology or redress, not from the individual at fault but from his government. And similarly, a family or clan would demand redress from the offender's whole group. If the offense was not too serious, the offender's group might collect cattle or goods and pay rather than start a feud. It would certainly do this if the offender had already proved to be an undesirable group member. Then it would exile him.

If the offense was murder, the offender's group generally felt the murderer had cause, and it would rally around him unless he was worthless indeed. Modern law demands the death of the murderer himself, but the injured family did not think in such terms. It had lost a group member, and it demanded that the other group lose a member of equal value. So if some worthless young man had murdered a chief, the chief's family would not be satisfied with merely killing any man from the other side; it insisted upon the death of a chief. But usually the offender's family would not permit its chief to be killed, and so an endless feud would start. There are stories among the American Indians about self-sacrificing chiefs who deliberately went out to be clubbed to death rather than allow their clans to become involved in a long bloody feud. However, if only an unimportant person had been killed, the family might willingly sacrifice one of its own unimportant members or at least exile him.

The Navaho Indians had this attitude, but the United States Army quite failed to understand it. Before reservation days, there was an army fort in Navaho country which interfered greatly with the grazing of the Indians' horses. During a scuffle over grazing rights, the Negro slave of the fort commandant was killed. The commandant immediately demanded that the Navaho turn in the murderer. The Navaho wanted peace, so they did what they thought was fair—they killed one of their own Mexican slaves and dragged him to the fort. They thought they had made honorable amends, but the commandant regarded the act as an insult, and a campaign followed.

The law of retaliation, *lex talionis*, was for centuries the only way of keeping order. Even when central governments began to develop, uniting clans or families under some sort of state, there was usually no police force. The only way to handle a murderer was to let his victim's relatives catch him and deal with him. At least they had an interest in getting him punished and would work without pay. However, they often killed too many people, with the result that the other side became the injured party, and generations of feuding followed.

To avoid these feuds, a high chief or the government would try to induce the injured family to accept a payment instead of a life. Each village of the Fox Indians was

headed by a peace chief. The chief had no real power to
enforce law and order, but when one family was about to
apply the *lex talionis* to another family, he would go and
plead with it. Sometimes he even had himself bound as a
captive, ready to die for peace. He would beg the victim's
family to smoke the peace pipe, and after the fourth request it was practically bound to consent. Then the murderer's family paid an indemnity and sometimes exiled the
murderer as well.

Gradually the paying of an indemnity came to take the
place of the law of retaliation. The Anglo-Saxons called
this payment *wergild*—the value set on a man's life. It was
collected from the whole family group, and some groups
even had rules as to which relative should pay the most.
The knowledge of what penalty might lie before it was a
powerful incentive for the family to keep its turbulent
members in order.

The providing of social life, education, and policing
were not the only functions which clans and large families
performed. They were very important to the economic life
of their members, taking care of the indigent and the
orphans and helping those who needed a bride price or an
indemnity.

It was no wonder that in many parts of the world clans
sometimes grew to huge proportions. It is clear that
they were almost essential in days when there were no
central governments or only weak ones. Sometimes they
lasted long after a peaceful government was established;
this seems to have depended on their usefulness and
peacefulness. If they insisted on the *lex talionis,* the gov-

ernment regarded them as a nuisance, as the Anglo-Saxons
did in King Alfred's day. If they exercised only peaceful
functions, such as aiding the indigent and keeping watch
over their members, the government might be glad to use
their help. This was the case in China. In India also, the
family groups, which finally developed into small castes
within the four main castes, were the chief means of keeping order during centuries of conquest and turmoil.

In the history of Rome we find another example of clans'
existing for some time after a central government had
developed. There the clans kept some power until about
A.D. 600. Many of us have heard of the extreme power of
the Roman father, who had the right to kill his son if he
chose. Actual accounts show that this choosing was not a
personal matter. He sentenced his son only for a grave
offense, and before he did this he would consult a council
of the *gens* or clan. This power was given to him by the
state as its way of keeping order in the days when the state
was young and without its own police force.

Clan power in Europe faded away as the Christian
church gained in authority. In order to put a stop to feuding, the Church ruled that there should be no marriages
closer than the seventh degree of relationship. It was
thought that this would prevent two powerful clans from
constantly intermarrying and thus forming a close alliance.
In addition, the Church was afraid that an unusually
powerful family might threaten its own rule. But even
without regular clan organization, powerful father-
descent families continued to exist. The Medici and the
Sforza in Italy, the Guises in France, and the houses of

York and Lancaster in England are all examples of these well-known families. For centuries a young man could scarcely hope for a career unless he was a member or a retainer of some great family. The only other ways he could further himself were by winning war booty or receiving a gift from some great nobleman. Rulers and even popes showered offices on their relatives, since powerful family members were expected to take care of their own. Today we are likely to judge this practice by our own standards, but there were reasons for this behavior then that do not exist today.

In most modern countries the usefulness of clans, and even of the big, close-knit family, is long past. Their roles in police duty, education, economic help, and social contacts have all been taken over by the state or by other agencies. The extreme obedience that families once commanded is now given to the state and the church. One who puts his family's welfare above the welfare of the state is considered irresponsible. Still, it is well to realize that the family was the seedbed out of which wider responsibilities grew. Perhaps in time national responsibilities will also grow into world responsibilities.

CHAPTER 4

Choosing a Mate

Back in the Middle Ages the Duke of Bavaria said to his fifteen-year-old daughter, "Belle (fair one), I have given you a husband."

"Blessed be God," said the fair one.

A generation ago, outside a mud hut in Arizona, a Papago Indian told his daughter, "My child, we are going to marry you tomorrow."

"Yes, my father," said the maiden.

Neither girl asked what her future bridegroom was like, or even what his name was. Strange as it seems to us, these were secondary considerations for them. The important thing was that they were now assured of a woman's job in life—caring for a home and raising a family. Of course it was hoped that the man concerned would be as agreeable as possible, but this wasn't something they expected or had any right to demand. Up until modern times, the consideration in marriage was not the individual, but the family.

We have already seen that families in many parts of the world were like little nations. They and they alone protected their members, furnished their livelihood, and governed their activities. It was vital to the family that anyone marrying into it should have desirable property, connections, and behavior. It was equally vital that when one of its members married, he or she should not swell the ranks of an enemy group. No wonder that the important matter of a family alliance was not left to be settled by a fifteen-year-old girl or boy. This decision was made by the person who bore the responsibility for the family fortunes—the parents, an uncle, or, in some American Indian tribes, the warrior brother. The family might be Arabian, its life depending on increasing its herd of camels, goats, and horses. It might be a family of Roman patricians, guarding not only its wealth but its precious ancestry. Or it might be one of the noble families of Europe, consolidating its power through marriage. Sometimes it was the boy's family who took the first steps in choosing a mate; sometimes it was the girl's. But in either case the father and mother, or perhaps a whole council of relatives, deliberated about the marriage choice as carefully as a modern nation deliberates before committing itself to a political alliance.

The first consideration was—did the mate stand in the

proper relationship to the family. Most groups had their rules requiring exogamy—marriage outside of the family group, and disobeying these rules meant a great deal more than family disapproval. It was a sin which would be punished by the gods or the spirits. Kipsigis in Africa thought the sinning couple would have no children. Navaho Indians thought they would go mad and jump into the fire. The black Arunta in Australia did the punishing themselves, to forestall spirit vengeance. The man who had married into the wrong "skin" had to stand still and have spears thrown at him, and the woman was battered with sticks by women of her own "skin."

In most cases one could not marry inside the stem family or the clan, even if the clan contained a thousand members, as some in China did. Oliver La Farge tells the pathetic story of a young Navaho who saw a beautiful girl at a ceremony for the first time. He fell in love with her, and then discovered that she was a member of his own clan who had been living off the reservation. He mourned, "What can be the matter with me that I should fall in love with my own sister!"

When a Kipsigi boy sees a girl who pleases him, he asks her immediately what foods she is forbidden to eat. Every section of a clan has some forbidden foods, and if hers are the same as his, he knows he must give her up. Sometimes even if the girl belongs to a clan section into which a boy may marry, she may be related on the other side of the family, and there are groups that prohibit marriage with some of those relatives also.

This prohibition means not only that the young people

must not marry, but also that they must not flirt with each other, or sometimes even speak to each other. Teachers at a modern American Indian school were distressed because the parties they arranged so often fell flat. Boys would stand on one side of the room, girls on the other, sometimes with their backs turned. "Indians are so unsociable," one young teacher complained. Then she learned that the unsociable ones were clan brothers and sisters.

As civilization advanced, and rank and wealth grew in importance, exogamy ceased to be the primary factor in marriage considerations. The Church, which had at one time forbidden marriage within the seventh degree of relationship on either side, relaxed its rule, so that anyone more distant than a first cousin was eligible. The previous rule had proved impractical, since it was easy to evade it by saying the relationship was not known. European royalty took advantage of this change in the Church's position, because even in the days when crowned heads were plentiful, it was hard to find enough husbands for all the princesses. It is said that by the time of World War I, all the royal families of Europe were related. But royal families had found advantages in the old Church rule, too. When a mate proved uncongenial, it was easy to dig up some relationship hitherto unknown and get the marriage annulled.

There was another side to the relationship consideration, for sometimes relatives were expected to marry each other. Endogamy, or marriage within the group—whether the group was the family, the village, the tribe, the church, the nation, or the race—has always been important to

certain peoples in marriage arrangements. Many groups have felt strongly about keeping their heritage free from outside mixture, and some feel that way today. There are still royal families who object to marriage with commoners. Some churches exclude members who marry nonmembers. Some states have laws against racial intermarriage. The family, large or small, practices exogamy. But the family is part of a larger group, such as the tribe or the nation, which desires endogamy.

The Ptolemys of Egypt were so careful of their royal blood that they could marry only their brothers or sisters, and Cleopatra had fourteen such marriages in her ancestry. The Incas of Peru and the kings of Hawaii also married their sisters, although they would never have allowed such a thing among their subjects. Only royal blood was regarded as being so precious that it could not be scattered.

The Arabs chose as a mate for a son or daughter a cousin inside the stem family, on the father's side. From her infancy an Arabian girl knew who the chosen man was, and if she preferred someone else she had to get her cousin's consent. This makes a very different kind of love story from the one in which the objector is the cruel father.

The classic example of endogamy is found in the caste system of India. There are four main castes: the priests (who may follow any occupation they choose but are the only ones permitted to perform public religious rites), the warriors, the merchants, and the laborers. The last three castes are divided into numbers of smaller groups, each with a hereditary occupation. Each caste, beginning with the priestly Brahmans, looks down upon the caste below it and will not touch its members or eat with them. All castes look down on the untouchables, who perform the meanest kinds of work.

Naturally these castes, and usually the subcastes as well, practice endogamy. An Indian woman of my acquaintance told me that almost from the day of her birth her parents began planning a good caste marriage for her. This was in the 1940's, but even then she did not expect to have any choice in the matter. Today the castes have been officially abolished. In a busy modern city like New Delhi, people wear European clothes and have jobs without regard to caste. And yet I was told by the Indian woman that even today no decent Indian would marry without his family's consent.

It is clear that the question of relationship was of the greatest importance to the family or group of elders in their discussion of marriage arrangements. After establishing the fact that the family of the possible bride or groom was one into which the person could marry, they considered a second question—what advantages did the family have to offer.

All during the married life of the young couple the two families would exchange gifts, help each other in trouble, and probably give more of their children in marriage. "We are glad to marry that family," an Indian girl told me. "Good field. Good corn." This girl was not the bride. Her girl cousin was bringing a man into the family, and he would be sharing his corn with his new relatives. Another Indian explained why his people arranged so many marriages between their women and the men of a particular tribe. "Lots of strong men there," he said. "They help us fight."

In the Middle Ages and even later, marriage was one of the few roads to fortune. A young man marrying into a poor or unimportant family might lose all chance of a career. So his parents, especially his mother, spent a lot of time and effort trying to find a wife who would increase his wealth and rank. In China, families employed a marriage broker to find a desirable girl and negotiate with her family. In Europe, noble families might begin to look around for a mate as soon as a boy was born. Children of powerful families might be betrothed, or even married, while they were in their cradles. An English story of the sixteenth century tells of a little boy whose family had to bribe him into going to church for his wedding by offering him an apple. He was so young that his wedding and his bride meant almost nothing to him.

Girls sometimes improved their social position by marriage. A lovely young thing might so charm a highborn lad that he would overcome his parents' objections and marry her. Romantic tales are full of such episodes, but they cannot have happened often. The lad's family would have been in the position of a nation that loses its chance to gain a powerful ally, and it would undoubtedly have used all its influence to prevent the match. Generally poor girls married poor men, and often they were better off than the rich and noble girls who were passed back and forth like pawns, according to the alliances their male relatives could make.

The third consideration in the marriage discussion was
—what kind of character did the young person have. As
with the other questions, the family approached this in a
very practical way. About a boy it was likely to ask, "Is he
a good hunter?" About a girl it would ask, "Is she
industrious and good-tempered?" Sometimes the family
arranged tests before venturing on the new alliance.

We can see how very important a marriage was to the
whole family. After the elders had made this most vital
decision, the younger members were anxious to know if
the new companion would be a pleasant helper or a drone.
Among the Zuñi Indians of New Mexico, women live in
the ancestral home and bring their husbands there. Their
sisters' question about a new brother-in-law is, "Is he a
good gardener?" The daughters-in-law of a Chinese

household would ask anxiously, "Is the new bride a good cook and embroiderer? Can she do her share of the work?"

The young person who was to be married would be very anxious to meet with the approval of the new relatives. The Papago Indian girl referred to a few pages ago told me how hard she had worked in her girlhood. "I carried water. I carried firewood. I ground corn. I wasn't idle a minute."

"Did your family make you work so hard?"

The girl was puzzled. "Why, no. I wanted to marry into a good family."

Not a word about falling in love! In fact, that would not have been possible, since she had hardly ever looked at a boy. After the age of seven or so, the sexes were brought up separately. This sounds like a hardship to people of our different habits, but we must remember that almost any pattern of behavior that is established in childhood will probably grow to seem natural. Girls brought up in a convent, girls who wore veils whenever they went out of doors, girls taught to lower their heads and look away when passing a man—all got used to such behavior. In fact, they never thought of behaving differently. In the same way, young people in many parts of the world grew up without expecting to find romantic love in marriage.

But this didn't mean that married couples never loved each other. On the sculptured tombs of knights and ladies of ancient times, we often see the couple pictured lying side by side, with the statement that they were loving companions all their lives. A Hindu woman, surprised at the American idea of love, exclaimed, "But how can one love a man whom one does not know! Love is more real when it grows slowly after marriage than when it bursts out suddenly beforehand." And an American Indian woman who had been given a husband at fifteen explained, "Of course I came to love him. We starved so much together."

In the past this slow growth of affection, which developed between two people as they came to really know each other, was the only kind of love looked forward to and desired by most young people of the world. This was what the best kind of parents hoped for when they arranged a marriage for their child. Along with the more practical considerations of the husband's character, the father, or sometimes the father and mother together, tried to pick a man who would make a suitable partner. They did not consider charm or appearance, as a young girl might do, but we know how little help those assets often are in building a happy relationship.

True, there were sometimes selfish and unwise parents, like the cruel fathers in *Romeo and Juliet*. If parents completely failed to consider their daughter's welfare, the girl had a hard time. So did the boy, if he was married to an unpleasant woman because of her lands and connections. It is also true that the ages of the pair were not always suited. As mentioned before, there were many cases of infant betrothal, both in primitive and more complex societies. Among the Australian natives, a grown man might admire a married woman with many children and ask that she give him her next girl as a wife. In this group, however, a man had several wives, and he was married to a grown woman in the meantime. In Europe, it was once common for a boy baby and a girl baby to be betrothed at birth. They grew up knowing that their home careers were settled. As mentioned earlier, an idea implanted in childhood can come to seem not only right but natural. There seem to have been few rebellions.

Very often a little girl was actually married to a boy or to an older man. These child marriages shock us today, because we picture a big rough man leading a small girl by the hand and starting her immediately on all the duties of a wife. Actually, child marriage was no more than a ceremony. After the girl's future was made perfectly sure, she might stay at home until she was old enough to become a wife. Or she might be sent to her husband's family, to be educated by his mother.

This was the arrangement in India, where child marriage was quite customary. The little girl grew up in her husband's household, getting used to all its ways. Ultimately, as a young wife, she would have no difficult adjustments to make. India now has a law against child marriage. The reason is not so much that the former custom was wicked, but that individuals there now want to choose their own mates, as they do in Western countries.

But was there never any romance or love-making among the young unmarried people? The fact is that at most times and places in the world's history there has not been the universal belief in the importance of young love that exists today. Of course first love must have burst out here and there, before the young person's emotions were turned into other channels, but parents gave little weight to these sudden enthusiasms. And love was not the absorbing interest that it sometimes is for modern young people, for girls and boys had not been taught to regard it as the solution to all their problems.

Besides, the young people had very little time to pine, fret, or dream. If a girl was to be married at fifteen, or even younger, she had to prepare for her tasks as a wife. This meant learning all the varied crafts of cooking, sewing, and housekeeping, and perhaps basketry and pottery as well. The boy had to become expert at hunting, fighting, or animal husbandry. Almost before they had begun to think about the opposite sex, they might hear their parents make the all-important pronouncement, "You are going to be married."

Some primitive people, however, made much more of

sex play and courtship than others did. If for one reason or another the marriage was delayed, there was time for some courting and love-making. The young Plains warrior had to procure his wife by giving a gift of horses to her family. It took a good many successful raids to capture the necessary number of horses, and he might be almost thirty before he could marry. Meanwhile, though he was not so improper as to speak to his future wife in public, he would play his flute where she could hear it, and perhaps whisper to her through the tent wall at night. Masai warriors in Africa could not marry until they had finished their tour of duty in the army, which sometimes meant fifteen years of service. During that time, girls were allowed to visit them in their barracks, where a kind of love-making very simi-lar to the bundling of early New England days was permitted. A good many cattle tribes and fighting tribes allowed love-making between boys and girls before mar-riage. But these relationships were always subject to the rules of exogamy and family choice. In some Pacific is-lands, some parts of South America, and other southern countries, there was even a kind of trial marriage. It also followed the rules of exogamy, however, and the final serious arrangements were still made by the parents.

Everything that has been discussed in this chapter seems very far from our present situation, where young people are sometimes surprised that the family wants any voice at all in their marriage choice. It is true that the powerful reasons which once made marriage a family matter have been swept away. With the emergence of central governments, families no longer operate as little nations, using marriage to consolidate their power. Modern young people can simply choose the individual with whom they would like to spend a lifetime.

To help them with this choice, a whole class of experts has grown up. These are the marriage counselors, specialists who sometimes are connected with schools and welfare associations or who practice privately. They are now taking over the task that was once handled by the family. Girls and boys with truly wise parents may not need the help of these counselors, but they serve an important role for many people. They encourage the young person to consider the character of his future mate more fully than the families of the past ever did. Instead of discussing the mate in terms of his value to the group, they deal with the specific relationship between the two young people concerned. They may ask, "Does your fiancé have personal habits which will annoy you? Can you change your attitudes so that these things will not matter?" These are the sort of questions that become meaningful when marriage responsibility rests with the individual, not with the family.

CHAPTER 5

Winning a Mate

"WE BRING the cattle for your child!"

The suitor's clansmen are shouting as they approach the Zulu kraal. They have been expected for days, and millet has been ground and beer brewed. The young people of the kraal rush out to meet them and playfully bar the gate. The fourteen-year-old bride-to-be hides in her hut out of modesty, and for the same reason her young man does not come to the village to see her. These cattle are part of the bride price—the payment that is given to the bride's family by the family of the groom. The arrival of each installment is as thrilling to the Zulu maiden as flowers and telephone calls are to a modern girl.

There is a friendly scuffle at the gate. Then the boys and girls from the suitor's village come tumbling in and proudly march their beasts to the cattle pen in the center of the kraal. Beer is brought out, and the young people of both villages feast, dance, and play tricks on each other. The girl's father, head of the kraal, stays in the cattle pen to look over the animals. He has bargained shrewdly for them and has already sent back one installment because the animals were not good enough. He feels he has a right to demand the best. After all, he is giving away a daughter who is a good worker, and who will bear children to increase another clan. He deserves fair compensation.

This attitude was prevalent among most of the father-descent groups. The amount of the compensation and the prompt payment of it were often decisive factors in determining who would win the mate. In looking around for a marriage partner for its daughter, a family might find several eligible young men with the proper relationship standing, good family connections, and acceptable character. But why was one person selected over another? In modern societies a young man interested in a girl wins her by spending time with her, by telling her of his feelings, and by making love to her. In primitive groups, a young man interested in marrying into a particular family also had to win his mate, but he had to prove himself desirable not to the young lady herself but to her family.

Sometimes he had to prove that he as an individual had certain skills. Sometimes, as in the payment of the bride price, he had to prove that his family recognized the worth of the young woman and that it was willing and able to compensate her people for their loss. Such payments were a regular thing among cattle people who, as we have noted, were usually father-descent groups with a keen sense of property. There was a belt of them through East Africa and South Africa, and every respectable family had its herd of animals, which it valued the way a modern family values its stocks and bonds. Here the lobola, or bride price, was paid mostly in cattle.

The Zulus bargained over the amount, but the Lovedu had a fixed price. The little girls of this tribe were automatically betrothed on the day of birth, but before they were given in marriage the family expected thirty different payments from the boy's people. It specified the time each payment was to be made and the kind of animals to be given. For example, there was a goat "for the cradle," which was presented when the child was born. Later, when she was old enough to pound corn, there was a goat "for the stamper." As the time of marriage drew near, there was a cow "to stop her mother's complaints," and finally, one for the father who had supported her. If the young man's family could not meet these payments, the girl's family might choose another mate.

Families were usually able to provide the necessary payments, and the wooing went smoothly. The cattle the girl's family received were used to enable its sons to win wives. The ideal situation was the marriage of a brother and a sister to the sister and brother of another family, for then no wealth changed hands. This was a favorite marriage arrangement all over the world, since it made a double bond between the two families without any expense. But suppose a young man had no sisters? Then he had to borrow from his relatives, and all of them expected to be paid back. Often he was unable to cancel the debt until he had a daughter of his own to bring in cattle. In the meantime, he and his wife were not considered truly married. Incidentally, if a young wife ran away from her husband, he then had the right to demand his cattle back. But in many of these cases the family had already used them to buy a wife for one of its sons, and the only recourse was to hand over this new bride to the deserted husband.

The custom of paying the bride price in cattle was not limited to Africa. On the plains of Siberia, wandering tribes kept immense herds of cattle, goats, horses, and yaks. Here a fierce Kazak tribesman might give fifty head of cattle for a bride. Our Plains Indians paid in horses. The bride price that an early Anglo-Saxon paid for a maiden was equal to the amount of cattle he would have had to pay her family if he had killed her.

Father-descent groups who were not cattle people had other forms of payment. In agricultural Africa, where the tsetse fly prevented keeping cattle, the bride price was often paid in iron hoes. On our north Pacific coast it was paid in furs and seal oil, and on many islands in the South Pacific, in shell money. The people of Manus, an island off New Guinea, made the price in shells, dog-teeth, and beadwork so high that a husband was sometimes in debt all his life.

The Yurok Indians of northern California paid with strings of rare, highly prized cone-shaped shells, called

Dentalium. A Yurok bridegroom scorned to bargain for his bride, but gave her family as many strings of shells as he could possibly afford, thus doing her honor. In fact, her social position and that of her children depended on her bride price. In a quarrel, one Yurok woman used to taunt another by saying, "Your husband did not pay as much for you as mine did for me!" A boasting child did not say, "My father is stronger than yours," but, "My mother cost more than yours."

People with little property did not make such high demands for a bride price. In many cases a simple present of food was satisfactory payment. Longfellow described such wooing in his verses about Hiawatha's bringing a deer to Minnehaha's father. Sometimes a poor man offered his service as payment of the bride price. The suitor lived with the bride's father and worked for him for as many years as was thought necessary to cover the amount of the payments; then he took his bride away. This was the arrangement between Jacob and the father of his two wives, as described in the book of Genesis. Some groups made this a regular custom, but the Yurok scornfully regarded it as a "half marriage," for until the bride price was fully paid, the children belonged to the bride's family.

In most of the above cases, residence was patrilocal, but there were many groups in which the groom came to live with his wife's people, at least for part of their married life. In that case his labor—usually farm work—would enrich her family, and it was not fair to ask that he earn his mate by paying a high bride price as well. That is why the matrilocal Iroquois Indian merely brought a load of venison to his bride, and the Hopi only had to contribute a special variety of corn.

Occasionally a couple grew rash and eloped. Life was hard then, and often after a few years they returned to beg their parents' pardon. If they were not in a forbidden relationship, the boy's family sometimes made an "honest woman" of the girl by giving her father some cattle as a bride price. But such elopements were very few, for it was almost impossible for a young couple to make a living on their own.

These bride-price customs are found in some primitive societies today. They were once characteristic of many societies of the past, but changes occurred as cities, social classes, large estates, and money came into being. Instead of courting the prospective mate with payments of cattle, shells, or food, the young man's family promised her a dower. This is a portion of the deceased husband's estate, and it can be regarded as an outgrowth of the custom of paying a bride price. The bride price often included an obligation on the part of the husband's family to provide the wife with a new mate if her husband died, but the dower assured her of money instead. Usually it was sufficient for a family to promise that the girl would be given a dower if she were widowed, but in Mohammedan countries the bridegroom had to declare the amount of the dower during the marriage ceremony.

During this same period, the custom of dowry emerged also. Dowry is a sum of money which a wife brings to her husband at marriage. Originally it was given to the man by her family to help support her, though it was not always used for that purpose. The dowry is an interesting variation of the bride price or dower, for here it is the woman's family that is trying to win the mate. To marry its daughter into a desirable family, the girl's family might have to provide a very high dowry indeed. This was the case in India during the time of British rule. An Indian boy who was educated in England was able to get one of the much sought-after government positions in his country, and he was considered a very desirable husband. A young Indian girl needed a large dowry in order to marry such a man. Dowry has played an important role in winning a mate since the days of ancient Greece and Rome. In the seventeenth century, the Earl of Salisbury summed up the attitude of many people when he said, "Beauty without dowry is like a gilded shell without a kernel."

The paying of a bride price, dower, or dowry was not the only way to win a mate. As mentioned earlier, the young man sometimes had to show the girl's family that he had certain skills. Remember the fairy tales about the king who promises his daughter's hand to the suitor who can slay the dragon? These stories are echoes of the widespread custom of asking the suitor to prove his worth as a hunter and a warrior. This demand was equivalent to the question asked by a Victorian father—"Can you support my daughter in the style to which she is accustomed?" The Makah Indians, whalers on the coast of Washington, demanded whaling skill as well as a rich bride price in furs and seal oil. A suitor, wooing the daughter of a famous

whaler, would come with his friends and camp outside the great wooden house which was the Makah dwelling. They would bring a canoe and drag it up on the shore. Then the suitor would stand in the canoe and throw harpoons at a board which had been put up as a target. If he could pierce the board from a great enough distance he was considered eligible. Other tribes on this wealthy coast gave suitors a whole battery of tests. They were rich and powerful, and they demanded the best for their daughters.

Sometimes the mate was tested after marriage. The Bemba, an agricultural tribe of South Africa, ask nothing of an incoming husband but work, which is done under the strict supervision of the old male head of the family. But this does not automatically give him the right to claim his bride. For some years the adolescent boy and his girl wife live as playmates. They are getting acquainted, say the Bemba. After the girl's maiden initiation, the couple live as man and wife, but they still do not have their own fireplace or garden. The girl eats with her mother and the boy with the men, as all Bemba do; but the mother-in-law, not the wife, cooks for the young husband until she feels her daughter is competent. It is a trial marriage which may last for ten years, and during that time either partner may end it if the other is unsatisfactory. Only when they have proved themselves efficient at housekeeping and gardening and have had several children, may they move out and start a home for themselves. In this situation it is not only the boy who is being tested, for if the girl fails as a housekeeper and as a mother her husband may leave her. Winning the mate is a challenge for both the boy and the girl.

Much has been written about winning a mate by capture, but among preliterate groups this did not take place as often as was once believed. In tribe after tribe we have seen how the family exercised control over the member's choice of a mate. Strangers were shunned, and there were strict rules about which group an individual could marry into. Tales of the independent, adult cave man grabbing any mate he fancied are myths.

In some instances feuds broke out between clans because of the stealing of women, but this could not have happened often. The offender who got his clan into trouble in this way was usually exiled, just as he would have been for killing a man. The Siberian herders, however, include a mock kidnaping in their wedding ceremony, so perhaps this was a custom of their warring bands in the past. As a rule, the systematic stealing of women in large-scale raids did not take place until groups were well organized and powerful enough for conquest. An example of this, according to legend, is the kidnaping of the Sabine women by the Romans. In these cases, the women of the conquered group were generally taken as captives, while the men were killed. The conquerors usually married these women, but often there was a probation period or a purification ceremony first.

We can see that these customs of winning a mate—by paying a bride price, dower, or dowry; by testing the skills of the husband as a provider and the wife as a housekeeper; or by capturing a woman—differ greatly from modern wooing. Romantic love was possible only when the individual, not the group, was the important consideration in marriage. And individual considerations did not become significant until the power of the family had lessened and young men were able to make their own fortunes in crafts, in war, and in exploration. Then young people could demand romance.

Poets and storytellers have taken up the theme of romance, and it now fills our monthly magazines and the fiction shelves of our libraries. And yet there are people in other countries even today who cannot understand our stories of young love. Just a generation ago, a class of

Japanese students who were studying literature told their American teacher, "Stories about devoted mothers we can understand, or stories about heroic sisters. But in the love story of a young girl, what is there of interest?"

CHAPTER 6

Weddings

THE ORGAN peals. The clergyman, the groom, and the best man wait at the altar, and down the aisle comes the bridal procession. This is a full-scale church wedding, the kind every bride is said to desire. Six ushers walk two by two in formal attire, with white flowers in their buttonholes. They are young friends of the bridegroom. Six bridesmaids, girl friends of the bride, follow. They wear matching gowns, the loveliest they, or sometimes the bride, can afford; and they carry flowers. Then come the maid or matron of honor and perhaps a little flower girl or a page. Last is the bride on the arm of her father, who will give her away. She wears a trailing white gown, and a white veil covers her face. She may be crowned with orange blossoms, and she, too, carries flowers.

At the altar, the bride and groom make promises of fidelity, his sometimes including the statement, "With all my earthly goods I thee endow." He places a ring on her finger, and the clergyman pronounces them man and wife. The maid of honor lifts the bride's veil, and the couple receive a blessing. Then the procession comes up the aisle in reverse order. In the vestry the bride is kissed by her friends and relatives, and then everyone drives to the bride's home. Often the wedding guests like to decorate their cars with colored streamers and toot the horns all the way.

The culminating act of the ceremony is a feast. It is the first time the couple have eaten together as man and wife, although a Jewish couple share wine at the altar. The bride cuts a cake. It is smilingly said that the cake has magic properties for any maiden who puts a slice of it under her pillow. She will dream of her future husband. Finally, the bride and groom go off together. She tosses her bouquet among the bridesmaids, and the one who catches it will be the next bride. Rice or confetti, and perhaps an old shoe, are thrown after the departing car.

This pageant, and the trousseau as well, has been arranged and paid for by the bride's family. Now the groom takes over. He has already given presents to his ushers and perhaps to the bridesmaids, and he has paid the clergyman's fee. Now he handles the wedding trip and finally escorts the bride to their new home. If he is truly conventional, he will carry her over the threshold.

This is a description of the well-known Episcopal ritual. However, every religion—Catholic, Protestant, or Jewish—has its own loved version of the marriage sacrament. As we go on to study other ways of uniting a couple, in various lands and at various times, we will find many features of this marriage ceremony appearing over and over again. Veils of red or orange, of silk, cloth, or leaves, have covered millions of other maidens entering the married state. The flowers and the rice are symbols of fertility, as ancient as marriage itself. The meal together, which some couples now omit, has been one of the most binding, and sometimes the only, form of ceremony.

Surprisingly, the use of a church and the clergyman's blessing are some of the newer elements of marriage. As we have seen, throughout history marriage was a practical alliance between two families, its essentials being a contract and a payment. In Europe the Church did not succeed in making marriage a sacrament until the Council of Trent (1545-63). Even today, by far the larger number of the world's inhabitants do not regard marriage as a sacrament, although they do call on the help of God, gods, or spirits at other important times—birth, maturity, and death. These, however, are times of dramatic physical change, and marriage is not. So, while the marriages we shall picture now had features similar to those of the Episcopal ceremony just described, they always differed from it in one respect—they were all civil, not religious, ceremonies.

Often they were very casual affairs. For instance, my Papago Indian friend's account of her wedding day was this: "My mother said to me, 'Now we go.' She took a basket of beans for a gift, and we walked to the other side of the village, where the boy's house was. He was out in the fields, but his mother was home. She said to me, 'We have spread the mat for you.' She meant the mat where I would sleep with my husband. So I sat down on it. The boy's mother gave my mother a basket of corn for a return gift. My mother went home alone with the basket of corn, crying."

Here the wedding procession consisted only of a mother with a basket of beans. Among other hard-working farmers or food gatherers, even that small ceremony might have been omitted. A Crow Indian family simply put a tepee next to its own for its son's bride, and he led her in. The farming Witoto of the South American forest sealed the pact without the bride's presence. Her father and the bridegroom merely licked a stick of tobacco together by way of contract and feast.

Simple marriage ceremonies are found among many of the tribes where the husband came to his wife's home. A Creek Indian bride's father said to the new son-in-law, "There is your bed. Lie in it," and the marriage was settled. But at the next Green Corn ceremony it could be dissolved if it had not worked. In Mississippi the Chickasaw bride and groom shared an ear of corn as a sign of their union.

The Navaho of New Mexico, at least in later days, took the occasion more seriously, however. I well remember the scene in a hogan—the earth-covered dwelling of the Navaho. There was a fire in the center, under the smoke hole, and behind it sat the bride and groom—she at the

north and he at the south. Firelight played on silver necklaces, earrings, and bracelets; for the bride, the groom,
and their families were decked out in all the wealth they
owned or could borrow. Each family was ranged at the
side of its child, in blouses of purple, crimson, and orange,
dark eyes glinting as bright as their silver earrings.

The act of union was the sharing of a bowl of corn mush,
the standard Navaho food. Across the top of it there was a
cross which had been made in corn pollen—a sign of
fertility—by an old man, especially chosen for his virtuous
life. Facing the east, the bride put her fingers into the
bowl of mush and ate a little of it. The groom followed
suit. Next, each of them ate while facing the south, then
the west, then the north—she first and he following.

That was the wedding ceremony which made them one.
When it was finished, all the guests ate from bowls of
mutton provided by the bride's family. Then there were
speeches, instructing the young people how to behave and
telling the bride she must always cook for her husband
and see that he was well fed.

Elaborate celebrations occurred among the rich whaling Indians of our Pacific coast. The father of a Makah
maiden, after testing the suitor and bargaining about the
bride price, was ready to provide an impressive feast. Both
he and the bridegroom sang ancestral songs, which told of
the great deeds of their families and themselves. The bride
was taken to her new home in the groom's canoe, an
enormous wooden affair with at least ten paddlers. She
was given a magnificent send-off. Her father had her carried to the beach in a canoe loaded with expensive furs—

her dowry. Among other whalers of that region, a bride walked to the beach over a carpet of furs, which had been given to her as wedding gifts.

On Second Mesa, as the whites have named one Hopi locality, it is part of the wedding procedure for the bride and bridegroom to prove their worth before the girl may take the boy home. Moreover, the women of his clan make a violent demonstration when he leaves. It may be that the bride or her family have done the proposing. The bridegroom's mother wants to know how good a house-keeper her boy is getting. So the bride comes to her home, and for three days she performs the daily task of all Hopi women—grinding corn on a flat stone. She is not veiled, but a curtain is hung in front of her, and she speaks to no one but her future mother-in-law. Meanwhile, the groom's clanswomen work up a righteous excitement. On the third day, they rush into the house, armed with containers of mud. They smear the house, the bride, and, if possible, the groom's father, whom they hold responsible for the marriage decision. This seems to be a rather unpleasant form of throwing confetti, but the women help to clear up the mess and return in the evening with peace offerings of stew.

Next morning the bride's hair is washed by the groom's mother and his by *her* mother. These acts are the high point of the ceremony, for the Hopi consider hair washing a solemn rite. On some mesas this is the end of the cere-mony, and the couple then go out to greet the rising sun. But on Second Mesa more ceremony must come before the two earn each other. Now the groom's kinsmen bring wool from their sheep. In the kiva, the underground room where they hold their clan ceremonies and spend their leisure time, the groom's male relatives card and spin the wool. Then they weave it into a square white mantle of ancient style, decorated with long fringe, as a trousseau for the bride. They also make her a pair of knee-high white boots, each requiring a whole buckskin.

This outfit takes twenty days or more to make. In the meantime, the bride, still at her husband's house, feeds all the workers, while his women relatives help her cook, and criticize her cooking as well. When the outfit is ready, she goes home, escorted by her relatives-in-law. This is indeed a wedding procession. Her father-in-law strews corn meal before her in the Hopi ceremonial manner, while her mother-in-law carries a gift of stew. Her husband, however, is not there. She has yet to pay for him. This is done with baskets and baskets of corn meal, ground by herself and her women relatives—bridesmaids, shall we say? Finally, there is a second procession, when the baskets are carried to the bridegroom's house with great display. Now he can come to his new home. He will not be, as the Hopi sometimes taunt a girl who has not paid for her groom, "living with her for nothing."

In Africa, among the wealthy cattle people, we find impressive wedding celebrations. But we must picture bare brown skin and leather kilts instead of white satin, and porridge and beer instead of wedding cake. One of the most elaborate pageants is held by the Zulus. It is preceded, of course, by cattle payments and, in this case, by secret visits of the bride to the groom. The final occasion is a three-day affair, filled with dancing and feasting. The bridal procession is composed of all the youths and maidens of the bride's clan village. They leave the home kraal at sundown singing, "I went off to marry and left my father. Yes, left my father." Indeed, the father, having already given the bride away, remains at home with his wife. He has no place in the girl's new life with another clan.

The bridal party marches, singing, into the groom's kraal, where they are greeted by all his clanswomen, crying, "Li, li, li! Better with us. Worse it is in the home of the bride." Now feasting and dancing follow, with the bridal party constantly refusing to do what they are asked unless given special food or gifts. The bride and groom do not eat together, however, for all food in the new home is taboo to the bride until she is thoroughly accepted.

The next day she is dressed in her bridal finery, which includes a leather kilt; ornamental ropes of beads or twisted calfskin; fringe at her neck, elbows, and knees; feathers on her head; and a veil made of strings of leaves. With her bridal party of boys and girls, she goes to the cattle pen, the sacred spot in the Zulu homestead. There, with much singing and dancing by her party and the groom's, she is presented to the groom's parents. Her own uncle prays to the ancestors that she might have "that which is red," a newborn babe.

Afterward, the friends of the bride and groom vie with each other in dancing and singing. An ox is slaughtered for sacrifice and feasting. The boys play tricks on the bride

and her maids and she on them. A night and a day pass
before the bridal party goes singing home, leaving the
newlyweds in the hut the bridegroom has built.

Among most African cattle people, the bride does not
usually wear a veil, but she may hide herself among her
maids or perhaps refuse to leave home until she is coaxed
and bribed. On the island of Manus she keeps her head
covered in the presence of the groom's male relatives during her engagement and throughout her married life as
well. Hiding used to be the proper thing for a bride in
Burma, sometimes even for the groom. Both had to be
coaxed out by their girl and boy friends, the Burmese
equivalent of bridesmaids and ushers.

The veil and the seclusion of the bride came into promi-
nence when money and rank became important. This was
the case in some of the father-descent Asiatic countries—
China, India, and the Near East. An American Indian girl
or an African girl was generally kept away from men, but
the rich girl in some of the Asiatic countries was a locked-
up jewel, delivered to her new possessor with great for-
mality and only after all payments had been made.
Accounts of married life in these countries often show as
real an affection as can be found anywhere in the West,
but the standard attitude is, or was, that man is the superior
and woman his modest and devoted helper.

A wedding day in one of these countries, therefore, was
not a day of regal appearance for the bride. In spite of
gorgeous clothes, bridesmaids, and processions, she was
practically invisible. It was the bridegroom's day. It was
he who paraded through the streets in gorgeous array, and

he who feasted, while the bride not only wore a veil, but remained out of sight until the last moment.

In parts of old China, after the bride's trousseau and the bridegroom's return gift had been paraded through the streets, the bride herself was taken to her new home with music, torches, and banners. The procession was as gorgeous as possible, and the bride was carried in a red sedan chair. But it was a closed box, with only a tiny grating through which she could peep out. In addition, she wore a red-silk embroidered veil. It was not merely a symbolic covering of gauze, however; it was a real covering, through which she could scarcely see. She had to be guided by two female attendants—her bridesmaids.

Halfway to the groom's house, she was met by the young men of his family. They escorted her to the great hall of his house and there, still veiled, she knelt with him before the tablets of his ancestors. Next came a visit to the bedroom, where the bed, sent by her family, was hung with bags of rice, believed to assure fertility. Only then was her veil removed, and the groom saw his wife, perhaps for the first time. They shared a symbolic meal, during which the groom ate all he wanted and the bride, out of modesty, ate almost nothing. Her modesty continued through two days of feasting—the first day for the men and the second for the women. During all this time the bride was on display in her most gorgeous clothes, but she showed humility in her new home by scarcely speaking or eating.

A bride in India was not always veiled. She was carefully bathed beforehand and dressed in red, the color of good luck, but she sat in one corner of the court of her

father's house while most of the ceremony was going on. I once saw such a bride, sitting with her head between her knees and her hair over her face so that one could scarcely tell who she was. Hindu stories joke about two men who exchanged brides by mistake, because they weren't able to see the girls' faces.

An old-fashioned wedding in a rich home lasted five days. The bridegroom dressed in a brocaded costume and wore a sword. After a number of ceremonies, he paraded through the streets to the bride's home riding a horse or, if possible, an elephant. He and the bride sat together while a Brahman dispelled evil influences. Then he tied a necklet of twisted gold threads around the bride's neck.

The necklet was the equivalent of a wedding ring and was removed only if she became a widow. Next the two walked seven times around the fire—symbol of the home, and rice was thrown on them. Then they ate together, for the first, and very often the last, time. Finally came the procession to the groom's home. If the bride was a child, she returned quietly to her mother, and when she was of age, the groom and his mother came to fetch her in another procession.

A Mohammedan bride need not even be present at her wedding. In Turkey an official and two witnesses go to the husband's home and ask him if he consents to the marriage. Then the official asks the same question at the bride's home. That is the ceremony, and now the husband goes in procession to get his bride. Other accounts from Mohammedans in India tell of the bridegroom's coming again in procession, to bring his bride home. He and his witnesses enter the courtyard of the women's apartments where the bride and her women friends are watching from behind a lattice. When the question, "Wilt thou have this man?" is asked, it may be the bride's guardian who answers for her. The wedding feast is luxurious, but the men and women eat separately.

Historically the traditions of our modern weddings in the Western world began in ancient Rome. But these weddings were not religious ceremonies. In accordance with Roman custom, an animal was sacrificed, and a diviner looked at its entrails for omens; but any friend of the family could do this. The ceremony was held in the bride's home, and in essence it was a civil contract before ten witnesses. Nevertheless, as a modern churchman ha

said, "Christian ritual has preserved . . . everything, down to the bridal wreaths."

The bride, it is true, did not wear white. Her cloak and sandals were of saffron yellow, a royal color. The upper part of her face was covered by a veil of flaming orange, and over it she wore a crown of rosemary, myrtle, or, a little later, orange blossoms. These growing things were symbols of fertility.

Before witnesses, the couple recited vows of fidelity. The bride's words, *"Ubi tu Gaius, ego Gaia,"* could be freely translated, "Wherever you are known as Gaius, I shall be called Gaia." In effect, she is saying, "Where thou goest, I will go." Next the couple ate together at a feast, and finally, there was the procession to the groom's house through the streets of Rome. The bride's hands were held by two little boys, forerunners of the modern page, and their presence in the procession symbolized the couple's wish for sons. Behind the bride came her maid of honor and two bridesmaids—one with a distaff and the other with a spindle. They typified a woman's housewifely duties, which were chiefly spinning.

Flute players went ahead, and the bridegroom and his friends followed, the bridegroom throwing nuts to the crowd as a symbol of fertility. All Rome joined the procession and sang gay songs. At their destination, the bridegroom lifted the bride over the threshold. He did this to prevent her from stumbling, which would have been a bad omen for their future.

Gradually the Christian church took charge of the marriage ceremony and made it a sacrament. This was a slow process, not really completed until the sixteenth century, for England and western Europe shared the ancient idea that marriage was a civil contract. In the days when the Anglo-Saxons were illiterate herdsmen, farmers, and fighters, the brides of the rich were paid for with cattle, much as African brides were. Also, as with the Africans, the payments might not be made all at once. The girl passed from under the hand of her father to her husband in two ceremonies. At the first, the bridegroom promised the *wed*— a payment equal to the amount which he or his family would have paid if he had killed a woman. This ceremony was the bewedding, later shortened to wedding. At the second ceremony, the groom made the payment. This fulfilled his part of the contract. However, there might be some argument about whether the bride's family had fulfilled its part. A law of the sixth century ruled: If a man buy a maiden with cattle, let the bargain stand, if it be without guile; but if there be guile, let him bring her home again. Perhaps the "guile" involved her not being a maiden, for a property-conscious cattle owner was usually very firm about his rights in a wife.

In later centuries, despite church councils and papal decrees, couples continued to regard marriage as basically a contractual agreement. They took each other simply by making a statement before witnesses or perhaps by having their guardians make it. England and Scotland even permitted a sort of common-law marriage, called handfasting or trothplighting, which didn't require any witnesses at all. A couple merely had to promise each other to live together and then do so to make them legally man and wife. Needless to say, they had little trouble in separating. Harold, the last Saxon king of England, put aside Edith, his handfast wife, when he decided to make a more practical marriage with a Frenchwoman.

When a formal ceremony with witnesses did take place, it was held on the porch in front of the church. This was not for religious reasons but because the porch was public. All the passers-by could then be witnesses, and witnesses were essential at a time when there were no written records. The bride came in a procession with a crowd of maidens carrying rosemary or sheaves of wheat. Do present-day bridesmaids realize that they, too, are carrying symbols of fertility when they carry flowers? No veil is mentioned, but the bride was dressed in her gayest clothes. When the two made their promises, the groom stated the amount he would settle on his bride. This was a survival of the old *wed* custom, and perhaps the vow in many modern ceremonies—"With all my earthly goods I thee endow"—is a relic of it. After their promises, the couple might or might not go into the church for a blessing. They certainly marched to the bride's home in festive array and ate together at a feast.

Very slowly a religious element moved into this ceremony. A priest was often desired as a witness, since he could write and make a record. The couple often heard Mass afterward, though there was no religious wedding ritual. By the twelfth century, the Church had ordained that marriage was a sacrament and that a priest was nec-

essary to bless it, even though he did not pronounce
the couple man and wife. There was an effort to have
announcements, or banns, called out in church on three
successive Sundays, so that anyone who objected to the
marriage could protest. France accepted the priest's services and, by the thirteenth century, couples there were
being married in church. In England, the clergy developed
a marriage ritual modeled, as many church customs were,
on that of ancient Rome. The ring and the veil slowly came
into use, although now the veil was not orange but white,
a churchly symbol of virginity. Still, many people clung to
the old church-porch customs, and although there were
churchly courts to judge such sinners, all they could do was
order penance. They could not break up the marriage.

Even after the famous Council of Trent had ordained
that marriage was a sacrament, which must be conducted
by a priest, England did not officially fall in line. In fact,
there were two hundred years of confusion, during which
there was never any real certainty as to whether a particular marriage was valid. Throughout the period there was a
contest between Church and State as to which should
handle marriage. As a result, there was a whirlwind of
arguments and statements on the subject, but no clear law.

This is an interesting period in the history of marriage.
With Africans, Indians, and Asiatics, it has always been
perfectly clear when a couple were married and when they
were not. When the bride price was paid or the contract
witnessed, the couple were married. Before it was paid,
even though the couple were living together, the contract

was not fulfilled, and they might part. But in England there were thousands of weddings performed with illegal wording or by clergymen who were not properly accredited. There was a scandal at the Fleet Street prison for debtors when clergymen imprisoned there began performing marriages for almost nothing, although they no longer had any right to do so. Besides, at a time when there were no regular licenses or records, it was easy to impersonate a clergyman and stage a mock wedding to deceive some poor girl. Many are the stories about girls coaxed into such false marriages and then deserted.

The confusion ended in the eighteenth century under Queen Anne. Banns or licenses were required, and the church wedding was standardized. At present, English marriages may be performed either by a clergyman or by a justice of the peace. Licenses are required and records kept, and they are filed at a central office in London.

Our New England ancestors, revolting against the Church of England, brought the custom of civil marriage to America. It was only slowly that church weddings, with their lovely pageantry, became popular here. The southern states were even slower to make the change. Now, throughout the United States, a license is necessary and sometimes a blood test, proving fitness for parenthood.

Today, even those who give up a great deal of the old pageantry still feel the appeal of such ancient symbols as the white gown, the ring, the flowers, and the meal together. There is a nostalgic charm, too, about the attendant youths and maidens, the wedding cake with its magic properties, and the thrown bouquet. And no matter what words are spoken at the ceremony, many a bride feels wholeheartedly the old Roman promise, *"Ubi tu Gaius, ego Gaia."*

FIRST WIFE   SECOND WIFE

CHAPTER 7

How Many Mates?

"I MUST take a second wife," said the Indian chief regretfully. "My old wife can't do all the work."

This Omaha husband had good reasons for his decision. As a chief, he was the welfare organization of his tribe. He was the loan bank and the hotel. He was expected to entertain any guests who came to the tribe, to help young men who needed goods in order to marry, and to take care of the poor.

To do all of these things he needed a great deal of help. Large stores of meat had to be dried; and many beaded costumes, beaded bags, and other leatherwork had to be made. More than that, to keep up his reputation he was expected to give great feasts now and then, at which many of these handsome leather articles would be given away. But there was no one to dry the meat, no one to make the gifts, no one to prepare the feasts, except a wife.

Today we might say, "Let him help with the work." Or, "Let him hire someone to do it." Or, simply, "Let him go without those things." But from the Indian viewpoint, none of these courses were possible. For a man to do a woman's job was as shocking as if he dressed in woman's clothes. Today, when women's work is often the same as men's, husbands do not have this feeling. But no people's actions can be understood unless we know their beliefs and values—their whole lifeway. As for hiring someone to do the work, that was impossible. There was no one to hire. Nor could the chief stop making expensive gifts or giving feasts. He would have lost his standing in the tribe and even his self-respect.

There was another reason for a second wife. Indians had no idea how to make soft and nourishing baby food. A baby's only hope for life was its mother's milk. In fact, when a mother died in childbirth and there was no nursing woman in the camp, it was thought necessary to bury the newborn child with the mother. There was no way to keep it alive. Children nursed for two or three years, and during that time both the father and the mother thought it wrong for a second child to be born, for it would take away the milk from the first. So the parents kept apart. If the husband had another wife, he could turn to her during that nursing period, and all the family understood.

There was still another reason for having several wives

or concubines at the same time (polygyny). When groups were small, every woman's first duty was to bear children to increase the tribe. If no eligible single man could be found for her, a girl's parents thought it best that she should go into the household of some married man. Of course, she went as his wife, and the children had an honorable place in the tribe.

In many tribes, therefore, a man would take at least two mates, if he could afford the bride price. If his wife had sisters and if he was a good provider, no payment might be necessary. The wife's parents would plan to hand each sister over to him as she came of age. They believed that the assurance of a good home for the girls was better than any payment.

In almost every part of the world, there is a saying that it is best to marry sisters, for they have learned to live together. There are tales of girls who objected to playing second fiddle to their older sisters in this way and who eloped with their own lovers. But there are other tales of two sisters' meeting a brave young hunter and begging him to marry both of them. A Papago Indian woman told me how pleasant this system of marriage was for a girl. Throughout childhood and youth, she said, two sisters had been together every minute. They hunted wild plants together. They ground corn meal together. They slept on the same mat in the earth-floored hut. When the elder left at fifteen to join a husband, the younger was utterly lost. She looked forward to nothing so much as joining her sister under the care of a man whom the sister found kind.

When a married couple live with a wife's family, sister

marriage is the only way for a man to have two wives. He can hardly bring a stranger into a home where his wife or her mother is the owner. Sometimes an overworked wife might even beg her man to take her sister as a second mate. Navaho Indian women have been known to request this. A Creek woman sometimes accepted a younger wife as a sort of servant. More often a Creek warrior had wives in different villages and spent some time with each. Incidentally, other matrilocal Indians, such as the Hopi and the Zuñi of the Southwest and the Iroquois of New York State, were strictly monogynous—married to only one wife at a time.

In some parts of Africa, polygyny really flourished. Here again there was a reason. Africa has some old and powerful kingdoms which once indulged in large-scale wars, and they suffered tremendous losses of men. During these wars, women were captured and added to the female population. In addition, Uganda and Dahomey formerly practiced human sacrifice and used men as the victims. As a result of these wars and sacrifices, there were so many more women than men that the African kings could have hundreds of wives. Even with lesser people, a man, by middle life, hoped to have paid for several wives to raise crops for him, make beer for ceremonies, and generally add to his status.

Among the king's wives at Dahomey were three regiments of so-called Amazons, outstanding female athletes and daring soldiers. In war they served as the men did. In peace they acted as bodyguards for the other wives whenever they left the king's dwelling. The other wives also had duties. The head wife, of noble birth, was the ruler of the women. The second had the important duty of cutting the king's hair and nails. Since these came from a person's body, they could be used for harmful magic. Therefore, they must not be allowed to fall into strange hands.

Some African groups still practice polygyny today. One visitor has described a prosperous Zulu dwelling in South Africa. There the homestead, or kraal, is a huge circular space, walled in with thorn bushes. Inside the hedge, at regular intervals, stand the huts of the owner's seven wives. Each wife has her own garden, where she raises grain and vegetables to support herself and her children and to provide food for the husband. He lives in a separate hut, where he keeps sacred objects, entertains guests, and talks with the male members of the kraal. In the center of the circle is a fenced area for cattle and goats. Each wife has a claim on the cattle that she receives as a bride price when her own daughters marry, and she can use them to buy wives for her sons.

The visitor reports an atmosphere of gaiety and companionship among the seven women, although naturally there are some lazy and jealous wives, just as there are outside polygyny. Their children call each other brother and sister. The husband visits each wife regularly and would be in trouble if he did not. Otherwise they see little of him, for he is occupied with travel and politics.

In many similar groups in Africa, the women get their pleasure from female comradeship, from work combined with singing and joking, and, above all, from their children. The husband occupies only a small sector of their lives. A group of wives have sometimes been known to gang up on a man and demand household changes, just as strikers might demand improvements from an employer. An African wife, brought up to expect this kind of marriage, was surprised when she was asked if she did not want a husband to herself. Her answer was, "It would be a great deal of work."

Large polygynous households, like those of a king or a chief, are, of course, exceptions. The most usual arrangement everywhere was one wife to one husband. Yet throughout Africa, Asia, and the Pacific Islands, we find that it was once thought perfectly permissible for a man to have as many wives as he could support. This was true even among the educated Mohammedans. There is a popular misconception that Mohammed gave permission for four wives. In effect, what he actually said was, "If you feel that you can act in equity, then marry such women as seem good to you—two, three, or four. But, if you feel that you will not do justice among them, then marry only one."

A good many Mohammedans had no more than one wife, and today the whole custom of having multiple mates is changing. But fifty or more years ago a wealthy man in Egypt, Turkey, Persia, or Mohammedan India might have at least four wives and, in addition, a number of concubines—women who live with a man but are not his wives. Both wives and concubines lived in special women's quarters, separated from the rest of the house. In Arabic this was called the *hareem lik* (women's place) in contrast with the *selan lik* (men's place).

In a wealthy home each woman had her own suite of rooms, where she lived with her children and servants. No men could come there except her husband, her sons, and certain other male relatives. When a festival was held in another part of the house, she could see it only by peeping through a curtain. In their luxurious rooms, furnished with cushions, inlaid tables, and rich hangings, the ladies occupied themselves with embroidery, music, and their beloved children. They went out, heavily veiled, to visit other secluded women and to spend their time gossiping, listening to music, and eating sweetmeats.

The life of the *hareem* lady appalls the modern woman, but is it really so alien? Today there are widows and single women who do not have male companionship, and there are married women whose husbands are too busy to go out with them. Large groups of these women spend their time at luncheons, teas, committee meetings, card parties, and literary clubs. Their conversation is generally about housekeeping, clothes, and children. Perhaps such modern women are not too different from the *hareem* ladies after all.

In China a man had but one official wife, and she shared apartments with her husband. However, she might have to put up with the presence of a concubine when her husband yearned for young companionship. If she was childless, she might even ask him to take one in order to continue the family line. Sometimes the husband took several concubines with the approval of his wife. Perhaps she preferred having her husband's new interests under the same roof, instead of wondering about them in ignorance.

Usually the concubines were like members of a female club—women who worked and gossiped and talked together. Their children had the same rights as legitimate children.

In America about a century ago, an earnest religious group, the Mormons, felt called upon to revive the custom of polygyny. They had reasons very similar to those of primitive people, for they were starting a new church and wanted all their women to bear children and increase its membership. Moreover, they wanted all these children to have fathers who believed strongly in this faith. With labor and heroism, they finally established their new group in the western mountains. They did, indeed, produce a population of loyal and energetic workers. But they were attempting to live in a nation whose whole life was based on monogamy—marriage with only one person at a time. The United States passed laws against polygyny, and the Mormons finally decided to conform.

Very little has been said about polyandry—having more than one husband at the same time. This custom has always been very rare, because few countries have ever had more marriageable men than women, and then not for long. However, there are certain circumstances, usually economic, which sometimes make polyandry practical. This was the case in Tibet. These mountain people were a father-descent group which paid the bride price in animals. A poor family had little hope of being able to provide a bride price for all of its sons, so the custom developed of buying a wife only for the eldest. He brought her home and allowed all his brothers to share his marital rights, although all children belonged to him. The others, however, continued to work hard. One by one, they, too, collected animals and were able to obtain wives and move out.

The Toda tribe, in the Nilgiri hills of India, have a more peculiar arrangement. The Toda religion revolves around sacred water buffalo, which can be cared for only by men. For this reason, girl babies were not considered valuable children, and many of them must have been exposed at birth. Anyway, the tribe seems to be short of women, and several of them have more than one husband.

We may wonder which man is considered to be the father of the children. The Todas have solved this problem by holding a little ceremony in which a man gives his wife a toy bow. After that gift is presented, all children born to her are his. But all the men want children, and presently the second husband is allowed to perform the bow ceremony and claim the next children she bears. Possibly even a third and a fourth man may do the same.

Does this seem unimaginable? When I visited the Todas, I saw clean little whitewashed huts on a grassy hillside. Before each one sat a woman in a white robe, with children playing around her. The men were away at work. It looked very much like a country scene in almost any nation.

An even rarer marriage custom is that of lending wives. An Arctic Eskimo cannot keep alive without a woman to make and mend the garments which keep him from freezing. So if an Eskimo is planning a hard trip and his wife

is unable to go, perhaps because of a nursing child, he and a friend will exchange wives for the time he is away. Eskimos, Australians, and other primitive groups who have little to offer by way of hospitality ask their wives to offer themselves to a visitor.

Polygamy—having many husbands or wives at the same time—sounds shocking and impractical to the people of the Western world. And indeed it would be impractical for us. Our religion and our laws forbid several mates, and we believe that monogamy is the best system of marriage. But we must remember that in our society there is a place for the single person of either sex. He or she can live alone in comfort and propriety. A single man who needs a cook can get the proper help without marriage. A woman today

can support herself and doesn't have to depend on a husband to take care of her. But in some parts of the world this is not yet possible. Dr. Albert Schweitzer, the devoted medical missionary in Africa, has stated that he will not speak against polygyny until some provision has been made for discarded wives. At present there is no place for them to go. In other parts of the world, polygamous customs are in the process of change. But the change must come slowly. Customs, laws, and religious ceremonies have become intertwined, like plants in a garden, and pulling one out violently may injure or destroy the others.

CHAPTER 8

Married Life

TODAY A NEWLY married American couple usually move into a home of their own, separate from their parents and relatives. They form an independent family unit and are fairly free to choose the kind of life they wish to lead. But in primitive societies a bride and groom were part of a large household, and the kind of life they had together was determined by the customs and needs of the family or clan with which they lived. Wherever families lived in close groups, sharing food and work, every member had special duties and was expected to behave in certain ways. The most important job of a new mate, coming into a household whose habits were already set, was to fit into this family pattern.

When a young Zulu wife settled in her new home after all the marriage payments and ceremonies, she was in somewhat the same position as a high-school graduate who goes to college and finds herself a freshman all over again. She had been thoroughly accepted by her own clan, because she had been a part of it for so long and knew all its ways. Now she was entering the domain of a strange clan, which regarded all other clans with some suspicion. At first she was not allowed to enter the cattle pen, the heart of an African kraal, for her presence there was thought to be dangerous. Nor could she eat clotted milk, one of the Zulus' most valued foods. In addition, she had to remain in her hut with her face veiled for several days after she came to the new kraal. This seclusion ended only when her mother-in-law made a feast for her, and the length of time she remained secluded depended on how well she fitted into the new family.

Modern couples often visit their parents and relatives. Sometimes they are more friendly with some relatives than they are with others, and their feelings toward different members of the family determine how often they see them and how they behave toward them. But as we have seen, primitive societies never left relationships to chance. They specified which relatives the bride and groom were to have close contact with, and which relatives were to be avoided.

A Siberian wife, living in the same huge tent with her husband's parents, turned her back to her father-in-law and even to her husband's older brother. She never stepped over their feet, never walked between them and the fire, never mentioned their names. This was difficult in a group where proper names often referred to plants and animals. A Kirghiz woman, forbidden to use the words *wolf, lamb, rushes,* or *water,* was obliged to say, when she saw a wolf running off with a lamb, "Look! The howling one is carrying the bleating one's young through the rustling ones on the other side of the glistening one!"

An Apache had to avoid contact with his wife's mother and sister. He was even expected to be distant and careful in his speech with her father and brothers. He especially avoided using any improper words in the presence of her father. A student of Indian customs once asked a young Apache husband to interpret the myths his father-in-law was telling. He refused to do so, for the stories contained coarse words which a son-in-law could not use in front of his father-in-law.

Sometimes both husband and wife had to avoid contact with their parents-in-law and even with other close relatives. A Manus bride in the South Pacific could never speak to her husband's relatives. This was particularly difficult, since she lived in the rear room of a house belonging to his brother or uncle. She used a different door, and when she went out she concealed herself from her in-laws in a long cloak. Her husband also had to avoid her relatives. Other examples of this kind of avoidance are found in Siberia, South America, and the South Pacific.

Perhaps the most frequent kind of avoidance, however, and one that is not hard to understand, is avoidance between the mother-in-law and the son-in-law. It takes place mostly in matrilocal groups, where a young husband suddenly intrudes on a household managed by an elderly

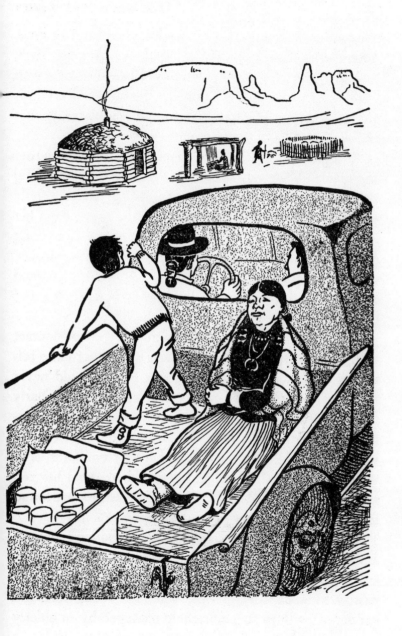

matron. Strict rules usually forbid their speaking to each other or looking at each other. If a young man sees his mother-in-law coming along a trail, he will plunge into the bush. Navaho Indian mothers-in-law once wore little silver bells to give warning of their presence. Nowadays, a Navaho husband sometimes places a canvas between the front and back of his truck, so that his mother-in-law may be driven to town without being in direct contact with him.

Many other groups among our American Indians and in parts of Africa, Australia, and the South Pacific also keep this official distance between son-in-law and mother-in-law. Yet, as is usual with rules of human behavior, there are some exceptions. Some mother-descent groups manage to do without avoidance, and some father-descent groups practice it.

Although avoidance is the name we usually use to describe such behavior, it is called respect by the people who practice it. Over and over again in-laws, both young and old, have explained that they have the kindest feelings for each other. When a Hidatsa Indian wanted to give a choice piece of buffalo meat to his mother-in-law, he would give it to his wife and say, "This is for that old woman." Although he did not even mention her name, he certainly had a friendly attitude toward her. In the same way, the mother-in-law would hand her daughter a pair of beautifully made moccasins for "that young man." Perhaps avoidance was a way of forestalling any quarrels between the family and its new member. But whatever its purpose, it was an important custom and one that the new mate had to follow.

Today a married couple spend a great deal of time with each other. They live together, eat together, and participate in many of the same activities, for we allow far more companionship between the sexes than there has been in almost any other society. In most primitive tribes, men had their recreation without their wives, and often ate apart from them. In many African groups, the women lived in their own huts with their own children. They cooked for the husband and sent the meal to him, but then they ate in their own homes. In Melanesia, the separation of the sexes was even more complete. There the men did not eat or sleep at home; they only came there to visit. They spent their nights in the men's clubhouse, which was secret and forbidden to women. Not only were women prohibited from entering the clubhouse, they couldn't even come anywhere near it. In Greece, Persia, and the Mohammedan countries, wives lived in their own apartments, completely separate from the husband. They spent their time with the other women, their servants, and their children, and saw the husband very rarely.

Every people, even our own, distinguish between men's work and women's work. Primitive groups have always had a clear dividing line between the two, but it has varied from people to people. Examples of these variations can be found among different Indian tribes today. A Plains Indian will refuse to do farm work. That is a woman's job, he says, and if he handles a spade he will be humiliated. Yet men in the Hopi and Zuñi Indian villages do all the farm work, while a woman's sphere is definitely in the home.

Our own culture thinks it is the duty of men to carry heavy loads. But in many primitive groups women do all the carrying, because men must have their hands free for weapons. Modern men have criticized such husbands and have received a surprised stare. Were they expected to do women's work?

In most places, the division between men's occupations and women's occupations put ceremonies entirely in the hands of the men. A number of tribes in the South American forest held ceremonies in the men's clubhouses. The Pueblo Indians in New Mexico and Arizona had an underground chamber, the kiva, where sacred ceremonies were performed, and women were admitted only at certain times. Among the Hopi and Zuñi there were also men's clubhouses, where men did their weaving and prepared for ceremonies.

Whether or not they had a clubhouse, tribes usually had a men's society which was forbidden to women. Sometimes the men's society had magic powers. Often it owned horrible masks and magic noisemaking instruments, such as trumpets or a sort of rattle called a bull-roarer. The women were told that the sounds of these instruments were the voices of demons and that they should hide themselves, or even leave the village, when they heard the sounds. There were such societies in Africa, Australia, the South Pacific, South America, and the Aleutians. In fact, men's societies dealing with ceremony existed almost everywhere.

In mother-descent groups such as the Hopi and Zuñi of Arizona, women did have their own ceremonies and

their own societies. In a few groups among the Plains Indians, women had societies of their own or, at least, joined a society with their husbands. But generally, ceremony was not their sphere. They seem to have been perfectly content to take care of the practical functions—bearing children, tending their homes, and feeding their men—leaving ceremony, as well as war, to the sex which had time for it.

The warrior's wife did plenty of hard work, but it was usually in the home and on the farm. Business and politics, as well as ceremony, were men's activities. But there are interesting exceptions to this. In parts of Africa, all the trading is done by women. In Russia not too long ago, the really admirable Jewish men did not engage in trade. Instead, they studied the Scriptures, while their wives kept shops and supported the family. We can recall a similar situation during the American depression of the thirties. Often men could not get work, while their wives, who accepted smaller salaries, had good jobs. It was only sensible then for the man to stay at home and take care of the house, while his wife went out to earn the living. However, there were many men who had nervous breakdowns under these conditions, for they could not stand doing women's work. Yet managing a house with modern gadgets surely takes as much skill as many kinds of factory work. And bringing up young children is certainly important.

Today the sharp distinction between men's work and women's work is fading in almost every country. In our own, mechanical equipment has so simplified housework that the modern woman often has little more to do than the primitive woman in her earth-floored hut with no dishes or furniture. Like the primitive woman, she may also help to support her family, although this support takes a completely different form. While the primitive woman contributed to her household by doing farm work, the modern woman now takes office jobs and enters such fields as government and religion. This development is very new, for throughout history, women, unless they happened to be queens or unusual leaders, have had little active part in government or religious ceremony.

Just as problems between a husband and a wife may lead to divorce today, so in primitive societies there were times when marriages failed. In any kind of marriage, divorce was usually possible, for the man. The wife's failure to bear children was the chief cause, but unfaithfulness could be considered a reason too. Divorce was sometimes permitted because of laziness and, in one African tribe, because of talking too much. If a bride price had been paid and the husband had good cause for complaint, he had a right to get his price back. Naturally the wife's relatives were reluctant to give up the wealth, and sometimes they had already spent it on behalf of some boy in their family. They would do everything to plead with their girl and discipline her, so that the difference might be patched up.

For a wife in a father-descent group, there was often no right to divorce at all. Her only recourse was to run away. If she could find a lover who would pay the price to her husband, all was well. If she had to run to her family, there would be a good deal of argument before they consented to keep her and return the bride price. But in clear cases of cruelty, the family might refuse to return the payment, and they might be backed up by friends and superiors. Where the bride price was small, a wife who returned to her family was not sent away. If she was healthy and industrious, her family could easily find her a new husband.

In mother-descent groups, the two parties generally had equal rights to separate and remarry. A Navaho Indian woman in our Southwest would simply put her husband's saddle—almost his only personal property—outside the door, and he would go back to his mother's home.

Marriage customs also determined what was done if the husband or wife died. The death of a wife didn't

seriously affect the situation of a man who was head of a polygynous household. But if a wife died without having given him children, a man felt cheated, whether he had other wives or not. He expected the dead wife's family to provide a substitute, and often he didn't have to pay another bride price. If the family had no available daughters, a cousin or another relative had to perform the duty, for the alliance between the families could not be allowed to lapse. A few tribes, notably the matrilineal Creek Indians of Georgia, supervised the widower during his period of mourning, before they presented the new wife.

The death of a mate was harder on women than on men. Those in mother-descent groups had the best of it, for an old matron might continue to rule the household, even without a husband. Early pioneers in upper New York State tell of an old Iroquois grandmother who lorded it over a whole village and was known as Queen Esther. In father-descent groups the widow, away from her own people, had a more difficult time. However, if she was of child-bearing age, she was still an asset to her husband's family, and provision was made for her. In Deuteronomy 25:5, it says, "If brethren dwell together and one of them die, and have no child, the wife of the dead shall not marry without unto a stranger: her husband's brother shall take her to him to wife . . . and the first-born which she beareth shall succeed in the name of his brother which is dead. . . ."

The levirate, or brother marriage, was practiced by the ancient Hebrews, the American Indians, and many other primitive peoples. Usually it was the younger brother who had the duty of taking the widow, for an older one was probably married already. The Creek Indians and several other tribes supervised the behavior of the widow before permitting remarriage, for the child bearer was family property.

If the head of one of Africa's polygynous households died, the son who inherited was expected to marry all the widows, except his own mother. Sometimes, as in brother marriage, any children of this new marriage were regarded as belonging to the dead man, not to the present husband. He, of course, had other wives to perpetuate his own line, for among these people children were the only real riches.

In more complex societies, there was much less emphasis on having a large family. The dead husband's relatives often demanded that a widow remain unmarried, even if she was a child, and spend her life in mourning. A Japanese widow was called by her husband's people a "cold-rice relation" and was treated almost like a servant. A Chinese widow was better cared for, but she, too, could not marry again. If she lived in virtue and obeyed her parents-in-law up to old age, they might put up a monument to her in the clan hall. In olden times, some widows hanged themselves in public and were much praised. The widow in India often threw herself on the pyre where her husband's body was burned. If she lived, her life in the home of her in-laws was practically that of a servant. She dressed in white all the time, wore no ornaments, ate only one meal a day, and never attended feasts. Philanthropists and, in recent years, the government have tried to find employment for these widows so that they could earn a living and have some life of their own.

Many modern people think these customs were queer and even cruel. Still, they were determined by the needs of the groups which practiced them and were very necessary for their survival.

CHAPTER 9

Increasing the Family

TODAY IT is not unheard-of for a young couple to decide before marriage that they will not have children. But in primitive times such a decision would have been unthinkable. People married for the very purpose of rearing a family to increase their group. Among the Bemba in Africa, a man lived with his wife's family almost as an outsider, until he had one or two children. Among the Papago Indians, he was not considered adult and fit to speak in council until he was a father. The Romans thought there was a curse on a childless man, and in India even a beggar might refuse to receive alms from him, fearing they would bring bad luck.

As for a woman, childbearing was her mission in life, and she was proud of her miraculous ability. The more children she could raise to adulthood, the greater her fame. In China, it was a mother of many sons who was asked to smooth the marriage bed of a young bride. Among the Apache Indians, such a woman massaged the limbs of a young girl at her coming-of-age ceremony. In old age, a woman's security and her social standing rested upon the number of children she had raised. One who failed to bear children was looked upon with scorn or pity, and almost everywhere this was a reason for divorce. Few people realized that sometimes the man might be to blame.

In most early societies, being a mother was a full-time job. A girl started childbearing in her late teens and continued until she was forty or so. A woman who wanted to rear a big family had to give birth to a very large number of babies, for in the days when life was hard and medical knowledge slight, perhaps half the babies born were destined to die. The use of charms to bring children must have been one of the earliest customs of the human race, for little statuettes representing pregnant women are found even in ancient cave dwellings. Special foods, special prayers, and, in later days, pilgrimages and vows were all used to gain this blessing. "O daughters of the king of the silver mountain," prayed a Palaung woman in Burma, "give me strength! Come love in abundance. Come pity. Do not forget me, O spirits!"

But the spirits did forget some people. Sometimes a woman was barren; sometimes all her babies died. Perhaps, however, a couple had some relatives who were willing to send a few children over to their house. If the houses were in the same village, the relatives might share all their children with them. Eskimos have been known to buy children from each other, not as slaves, but as beloved sons and daughters.

Because most primitive societies placed such a high value on having children, they often were less insistent on legitimacy than modern societies are. In several groups, having a child before marriage was an asset to a girl, for it proved that she was fertile. Today in Madagascar, if a native wife goes off with another man, her husband will demand that all children of the runaway pair shall be *his*. And in parts of Africa a wife's illegitimate children are urgently claimed by her husband.

When a woman knew she was to bear a child, both she and her husband were willing to go through all sorts of self-denial to ensure a happy birth. The woman's ability to produce a child was believed to be miraculous, and surely it is. Though we know every stage of the process, we still do not understand how a complete human being is produced in nine months from a single cell. Primitive people felt that the woman must be under the influence of some supernatural power. They also felt that this power might be dangerous both to her and to others. Often she had to leave her dwelling and go to live in a special hut, built to house women during their pregnancy and during their mysterious periods.

Men kept away from the hut and sometimes did not even look at it, lest the mysterious woman power take away their manly strength. The Papago Indians tell a story of one woman who was secluded in such a hut. It was located at the edge of the village and faced away from it. Looking out over the desert, the woman saw enemies approaching, and she tried to warn the men of the village by calling and waving to them. They saw her, but they turned their backs and moved away. They would have no dealings with her during her dangerous condition. Because they ignored her, their enemies were able to attack the village and slaughter the inhabitants.

It has been said that primitive women were secluded because they were thought to be unclean, but no Indians of my acquaintance regard pregnancy in this way. They feel, rather, that the women are in a mysterious and powerful state, raised almost to the rank of a spirit. Most likely this was also the attitude in earlier times. Men kept away from them as they kept away from all holy things—because the power of the gods is dangerous unless one knows exactly how to approach it.

Alone in her hut, the expectant mother could rest and be quiet. She had no work to do and could bend her thoughts to good things which she hoped would influence her child. Sometimes she took precautions to prevent the power that surrounded her from endangering others. This might entail using special dishes which no one else could touch and which were broken afterwards. Her food might consist of a special porridge or soup, brought to her by older women who had had children and who could not be harmed by her magic. These women might also help her when her time came. Among some American Indian groups, the expectant mother herself had to avoid con-

tact with the power within her. She could not touch her head with her fingers, for the head was regarded as the most important part of her body, representing the whole. Instead, she used a little scratching stick, perhaps a slender sliver of abalone shell, perforated so that it could be hung around her neck. Another ancient custom prevented a pregnant woman from touching her lips to water; instead she drank through a tube.

While her husband did not come near her during this seclusion, there were groups which felt that he and she were so truly one that the power surrounding her surrounded him also. Among some Indians of northern California, the husband too used special dishes, a drinking

tube, and a scratching stick. He did not hunt, fish, or fight, for this power would scare the animals and make him as weak as a woman. All over the world there are signs of this ancient belief. Papuans of the South Pacific islands forbade the husband of a pregnant woman to fish with them, to sail in the turtle fleet, or to hunt wild pig. The Bechuana of Africa would not have him on an elephant hunt, for he would surely be attacked. Among some South American Indians, he actually had to lie in a hammock, forbidden to take any action. Among the Basques, an ancient group in Europe, it was the husband who went to bed during his wife's pregnancy, while she continued her usual activities.

Many other people were not in such extreme awe of

the birth power. But there were a great number of groups which felt that a pregnant woman should not cook for her husband or touch his weapons. Among some American Indian tribes, men whose wives were pregnant held a special ceremony when they left their homes to go hunting. The purpose of the ceremony was to take away any harmful woman magic from their bows and arrows.

After the child had been born, the magic was still too strong for the mother to return home or go among people immediately. Most groups had rules as to the length of time she had to remain away from people, and it was usually longer if she had had a girl baby. During this period she was helped by women who washed the baby and, perhaps, used charms to take away evil influences. A native Australian woman lay in the bush, while mothers of healthy children sang songs around her. A wealthy Mohammedan lady lay in her gorgeous bed, while crowds of women came to call, bringing sweetmeats. They were careful never to look at the child, lest someone cast an evil eye on it. When they spoke of it, they discouraged the interest of evil spirits by such remarks as, "What a homely little creature! It will never grow up!"

When all was safe, there was a ceremony, bringing the mother and the child back to daily life. The Jewish mother brought a lamb or turtledoves to the high priest, who sacrificed them for her. In the Anglican church a woman gave prayers of thanksgiving for her safe delivery. This was known as the churching of women. Many Southwestern Indians took the child out at dawn, to present it to the sun. Among the Omaha Indians, a priest stood at

the door of the tepee and introduced the child to the whole world of nature by saying:

"Ho, ye Sun, Moon, Stars, all ye that move in the heavens,
I bid you hear me!
Into your midst has come a new life.
Consent ye, I implore.
Make its path smooth. . . ."

He also prayed to the winds, the hills and valleys, the birds, and even the insects, asking that the child be allowed to travel safely beyond all the four hills of life—infancy, youth, middle age, and old age.

These were the customs followed by earlier people if all went well. But there were many dangers that might prevent a baby from ever coming forth from seclusion. In the first place, the mother might die. This didn't happen too often among women who kept their muscles active up to the last minute. But it was a danger in later groups, where women took to their beds and lay there, awaiting the great event. Nowadays modern doctors ask expectant mothers to keep on their feet, just as primitive women did, for they realize that this will make childbearing easier. If a mother did die, however, there would be no milk for the baby. Occasionally there might be another nursing mother who was able to feed the child, but if there wasn't it was felt that the baby had better be buried with his mother, rather than die pitifully of starvation.

Sometimes the infant died at birth. This was always a possibility if there was difficulty in the delivery, for there were no trained people to assist the mother. Incidentally, Indians on the coast of Washington comfort themselves with the idea of a children's heaven, where baby souls go if their bodies die before growing up. The mother who has lost a child hopes that the same little soul which has left her will come back in a new baby body.

Even if the mother or the infant did not die in child-birth, conditions might be so hard that there was no hope of rearing the child. An Eskimo baby who was born in a stormy winter, when the hunters could get no food, was doomed from the start. The whole family would have to be on the move, searching for food, and the child would have to be carried on a freezing trip by a mother almost too weak to walk. Indians of the California desert, who trekked over hot wastes, feeding on seeds and lizards, had the same problem. Infants rarely survived these hard, food-seeking journeys, and therefore they were sometimes killed immediately.

Whenever a group was faced with a food shortage, the newborn child was likely to suffer. Even if the mother could keep him alive beyond infancy, she would eventually have to take food from her other children in order to feed the new one. Perhaps they would all sicken. So she often decided to give up the newborn life right away, before the inevitable food problems arose. This sacrificing of the weak newborn baby for the sake of the other children sometimes seemed necessary to more complex societies also. When Athens was in a state of siege, Athenian families made a habit of laying the babies they could not feed on the Acropolis, where some family which had food might rescue them. In most cases the baby relinquished was usually a girl, for a boy's eventual contribution to the family and tribe made immediate sacrifices more worthwhile.

Sometimes infants were killed for reasons other than a lack of food. The desert Arabs were fierce fighters, and their need of men was desperate. An Arabian baby had no place in the world until he was laid before his father, who spoke the word that would permit him to live. For many a girl baby, this word did not come. The father hoped that if his wife had no child to nurse, she could soon become pregnant again. Next time she might have a boy.

The necessity of sacrificing the individual for the good of the tribe also demanded the giving up of children who were deformed and who could never do their part in the hard life of the group. Deformities were not merely physical things, such as a crooked back or a club foot. Some tribes feared twins as being something unnatural, and they killed one or both of them. Others waited until the child's teeth came in and refused life to a baby whose teeth arrived in what they thought was the wrong order. Primitive people believed that these deformed children were not human, and, therefore, their presence was a danger to all.

The killing of infants occurred among groups which had no medical knowledge, no warm beds, and no baby food. When a primitive parent decided to sacrifice his child, he suffered in the same way that a modern parent suffers when he decides to let his child undergo a painful operation. It was heartbreaking, but it was necessary.

Once the baby was accepted as a member of the family, he was treated with loving care. For the first two or three years, he lived on his mother's milk, which was given to him whenever he wanted it. Later on, the mother might chew some of the tough meat or roots eaten by grown people and start the baby on this soft food, just as some birds do with their nestlings. The idea of regular feeding hours, once so popular with our doctors, was unheard-of. Most mothers kept their babies with them constantly, so that they could be fed the moment they cried. Zuñi Indian women were horrified at hearing of a white woman who left her infant for a whole evening with only a baby sitter, who could not nurse him. "But suppose he was hungry!" they exclaimed, aghast.

In warm countries a baby needed no clothes. He was carried naked, astride his mother's hip or against her back, slung in a cloth which was tied over one shoulder. Whenever he cried, he could easily be slung to the front for contented nursing. African women would even dance all night with babies on their backs, with both the baby and the mother feeling quite comfortable.

Many peoples bound the baby tightly in swaddling bands or on a cradleboard. The swaddling bands, used by the ancient Hebrews and many early Europeans, were lengths of linen wrapped around the body from ankles to armpits. Of course, they were often washed and changed. Their purpose was to keep the baby's spine from injury as he was handled, and to make it grow straight.

The cradleboard, used by American Indians, had the same purpose. Usually it was a flat piece of board or basketry, a little longer than the baby's body, and perhaps covered with buckskin. The baby was laid on a soft bed of moss or shredded cedar bark, which could be changed like a diaper, and lacings were passed to and fro across his body to hold him in place. A strap at the top of the cradleboard passed over the mother's forehead, so that she could carry the little one just as she did her loads of firewood. In fact, the baby sometimes rode on top of the firewood, where he hung securely, looking out at the world.

Babies were frequently taken off the cradleboard to be washed and, later, to try walking. Experts who have studied the physical effects of the cradleboard say that such babies walked quite as soon as those who could kick whenever they pleased. And babies seem to have liked its safety. At two years old or more, they have been known to cry for the board when they wanted to take a nap.

Parents did all they could to make their child a handsome member of the group. This often involved changing his physical appearance. The bones of a baby's head are soft and can be pushed into different shapes. The Maya Indians of Yucatan tied a pad on the child's forehead, so that it slanted back in a straight line with the nose. The Idaho Indians forced his head into a tall, peaked shape, while others preferred a head that was flat and broad. These alterations of the human body were regarded as very attractive by people who could not rely on clothes for decoration.

A baby was usually the pet of the whole large family, and he was always in someone's arms. Most primitive people did not keep count of the years and, therefore, could not celebrate birthdays. But there were many special events in the life of a child. The Coeur d'Alene of Idaho held a little ceremony for an infant's first smile. The proud father in Bougainville, in the South Pacific, took him to see the pigpen at a certain age, then to the opossum hunt, and, finally, to the men's clubhouse.

In addition to both the natural feelings of parental love and the value of a new healthy member to a primitive society, there was another reason why many tribes treated babies with such great care. Most primitive people knew about the process of childbearing, for they had seen it happen with animals. They realized that both a male and a female were necessary to produce a child's body. But his soul was a different matter. Many groups all over the world thought that the soul of an ancestor was reincarnated in a child, at least to begin with. As the little one grew, he would develop a soul of his own, but at first he could hardly survive without some stronger soul to hold the little life to the body. Some aborigines in Australia believe that the ancestor soul enters a woman as she passes a sacred spot. With accompanying ceremonies, the child's totem or sacred ancestor is decided for life.

The ancestor soul had to be treated with a good deal of respect until it faded away. The explorer Stefansson tells of traveling with some Eskimos whose small son housed an ancestor soul. Their dogs had died, and the men were pulling the sled with great effort, while the Eskimo woman walked alongside it. But the child was allowed to ride comfortably on the sled. He was not sick or tired, however,

for whenever the men stopped to rest, he would slide down snowbanks with all the energy in the world.

"If the child feels so vigorous," said Mr. Stefansson, "couldn't he walk and lighten the load?"

The Eskimos were horrified. They could not ask that of a revered ancestor.

Modern Americans often feel that primitive women had hard and limited lives. They have the same attitude toward women in other countries today, where wives still feel that bearing children is their most important function. When I have spoken with these women, however, I have found they were quite content. In fact, American wives who spent their time at such barren tasks as office work usually amused them. They regarded these activities as the playthings with which men kept themselves busy, while women went about the more vital task—bringing new life into the world.

CHAPTER 10

Names

"I KNOW it as well as I know my own name!"

When we use this expression, we are saying that we know something very well indeed, for our names were among the first things we learned to speak and to recognize. We hear them, say them, write them, or read them twenty times a day. A person who could not use his own name would be constantly confused and frustrated. Yet there are people in the world who never use their names and who would be shocked or offended if they heard them used by others. To them a name is not merely a form of identification, as most of us regard it. It can be a magic spell, an award of honor, the title of a chapter in one's life.

Many primitive people believed that a name was an actual part of a person and should not be handled without his consent. They would never consider speaking a name freely, as though it were everybody's possession. To use a man's name was to have power over him, in the same way that witches had power over evil spirits after they had learned their secret names.

A baby was usually named when his mother came out of her seclusion. Before that, the little creature did not really exist. One African tribe thought that if the baby died nameless, he was only a ghost child, sent to deceive the mother. The Mohammedan father whispered his baby's name in his ear when he decided that he should live. The Haida Indians of British Columbia bent over the newborn infant and called out different names until the child moved or made a sound. This meant that his name had been recognized. Later, if the baby became ill, they would decide that he had been given the wrong name and was uncomfortable. Then names were called again, until the right one was found. In Christian churches the baby is given a name when he is baptized, and the Calvinists once taught that he would not go to heaven without this baptism.

Modern couples often call on godparents to give their child a name with happy or dignified associations. This custom of calling the child something that might help him achieve success in life has existed since early times. Some American Indians asked the medicine man to give the child a powerful name from his dreams, and this name was sometimes so sacred that it could be mentioned only at crises in the person's life. Buffalo-hunting Plains Indians asked a famous warrior to name their baby boy or girl after some great deed he had done. The child was then called something like Arrow in the Throat or Bad Heart Bull. In recent years Indians have had a problem in translating these names so that they would keep their native flavor and yet be usable in modern business. Often they have allowed their white teachers to choose a new name and have accepted anything from Alexander Hamilton to Huckleberry Finn.

Some Indian clans had lists of names, perhaps describing their totems. A baby born into the Omaha Buffalo Clan might be called Short Horns or Running Hoofs, if no one else was using that name at the time. Some families had sacred names from mythology, which they owned and which no one else dared use. For example, a whaler's baby might be called Deep Under Water. An Iroquois baby might be given one of the great family names of his house, and this name would some day make him a candidate for the council of sachems. Sometimes a child was given no name at all until he was old enough to deserve one. Meanwhile, he was jokingly known by some baby name, such as Dirty Face or Crooked Legs.

Whatever the child's name was, he did not hear it spoken very often. Psychologists today tell us that the way a baby learns to know himself is by constantly hearing people use his name: "Johnny is a good boy." "Johnny, don't slap Betty." "Johnny, kiss Aunt Lucy." But the primitive child heard nothing like this, for his name was rarely mentioned. Nor was the name of anyone else. What he

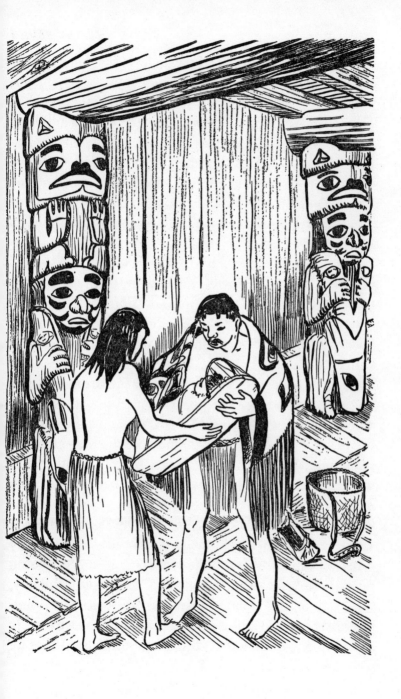

probably heard was: "My child is a good boy." "Brother, don't slap Sister." "Nephew, show respect to Father's sister." The words for these relationship terms were short and easy to learn, and the child heard them over and over again. As a result, he did not think of himself as a person with a name, set apart from all the others. He was child, brother, nephew, and as such he owed special duties to the various members of the big family. This ancient method of binding kinsfolk together was a powerful one, and many peoples still make full use of it.

Though a child's name was not used in speaking to him, some groups used it in speaking about his parents. A proud young couple in Borneo, who had advanced to adulthood with the birth of their first child, might be called Father or Mother of So-and-So. In various South Pacific islands and among many American Indians, this practice is well known. It binds the core family together and emphasizes the value of rearing children. There is an echo of this old custom today among some old-fashioned American couples, who address each other as Father and Mother.

The names of adults were not used any more freely than the names of children were. Among most groups there were certain relatives who rated special respect, and this was shown by never using their names at all, even when speaking about them. In primitive tribes a young husband who came to live with his wife's people was usually forbidden to mention the name of his mother-in-law, either in her presence or out of it. Even the relationship term might be thought too forward, and he would respectfully refer to her as "that woman." Had he dared to speak her

name, she might have been as insulted as though he had
sworn at her. Chinese families still follow the custom of
ranking each family member according to age. To our ears
it sounds awkward to say, "Second Uncle, are you going
out today?" or, "Fourth Sister-in-law, will you pass the
rice?" But in Chinese these terms are short and easy to
use.

Besides using a term of relationship, another way of
designating a person without speaking his name was to
give him a nickname. We still do this with baseball players
and even gangsters. Today, boys at school call each other
Slim, Carrots, or Lefty, and often their real names are
practically forgotten. In the same way an American Indian
might be dubbed Gourd Head, or Lame Foot, with no
regard for his feelings. However, these were not forbidden
names but convenient descriptions, and real names were
always treated with the greatest respect. Incidentally,
these nicknames were also applied to white officials, who
were not expected to take offense when they were called
Owl Eye or Big Belly.

Sometimes the respecting of a name went so far that it
was even thought wrong to use words that sounded like it
or formed a part of it. This was especially true of names of
the dead. It was feared that if a dead person heard his
name, he might think that he was being called and return
to trouble the living. In the state of Washington, Indian
languages changed unaccountably from place to place, so
that words that were common in one were never heard in
another. These words turned out to be parts of names like
Swift Elk or Salmon Fisher, which had belonged to re-

spected chiefs who were now dead. None of these four words could be spoken again until all who remembered the chiefs were gone. So, instead of *salmon*, people might say, "that which leaps in the rivers," and instead of *elk*, "the tall horned one."

If members of the family had to avoid using names, strangers were expected to be even more careful. Most primitive groups felt that it was an offense to ask a person his name or to address him by it. Sometimes a third person might be allowed to speak the name, but this was not permitted very often. Modern census takers, who are supposed to get the names of every individual in a dwelling, often have to give up in despair. If forced to give their names the people may institute a riot, because of the injury done them. We are told that the ancient Hebrews objected to being "numbered." Was this, perhaps, because of the registration of their names?

Name respect was practiced not only by primitive peoples. Until recently, a Mohammedan or East Indian wife was never expected to use her husband's name, although he might use hers. And in England a few hundred years ago, wives addressed their husbands as Mr. So-and-So, even when they were alone together. The terms Mr. and Mrs., once Master and Mistress, are our respectful substitutes for using a person's first name.

The first name, middle name, and surname which most of us have are a recent possession as world history goes. In the past, people usually had only one name at a time. Simple societies did not even have titles, such as Lord, Sir, Captain, or Doctor. However, Africans sometimes added a descriptive "praise name," such as Spiller of Blood. Other people changed their names, thus indicating a new personality, another chapter in their lives. Among some groups this was done regularly when boys attained maturity. A Creek Indian youth was publicly renamed after his first

war party. As his achievements as a warrior increased, he might hope to win other names, the way his descendants can now win academic degrees. A Plains Indian might get the boasting title—Young Men Are Afraid Even of His Horse. A Melanesian might take over the name of a slain enemy as a valuable piece of loot.

Our government had much trouble with American Indians who became soldiers and, quite naturally, changed their names with their new functions. A man with a heroic record might think that several changes were necessary. He had to be persuaded to take a "paper name"—one name that would be used consistently for signing checks and allotment papers.

Even people with no exploits to their credit often changed their names, hoping that the change would improve their luck. Among some American Indians, two friends might exchange names as a token of friendship. A man might even buy a name. I remember one Indian purchasing the name of Big Crazy. Women, on the other hand, did not change their names. They sometimes received a new name on attaining maidenhood, but after that their exploits were all of one kind. The only title they could expect was that of Mother of So-and-So.

In Europe, names were not secret, nor were they treated with such extreme respect. But, as with the peoples just described, an individual living in a small group, where everyone knew who his relatives were, needed no family name. In England, a person originally was called by some descriptive name, like Arth or Arthur, which meant noble. In Christian times, he might have had a name from the Bible, like John or Thomas. To this might be added the name of his occupation or his dwelling. These were names like Smith or Wheelwright, or names ending in -ton (town) or -wick (small bay). There were also nicknames, like that of the second Norman king, William Rufus (the redhead), or battle names, like William the Conqueror.

Sometimes a man identified himself as John-his-son (Johnson), but his grandson might be called Albertson.

It was not until the late Middle Ages that Europeans began to move about and live with strangers. Then they needed to proclaim their family relationships, not only for identification but to show their title to property. Aristocrats began to use the names of their estates, so that a Norman grandee might call himself Walter Dubois (of the wood). Then poorer people followed suit, and the Johnson family kept the same family name from generation to generation, no matter how many Wills and Toms there were in the line.

Names had a similar history in ancient Rome. At first Romans had only one name, like Romulus. Several centuries later, they had as many as three. Almost every man, especially highborn men, had a first name (Gaius), a clan name (Julius), and a family name (Caesar), which was perhaps once a nickname. Caesar's adopted son had the "praise name" of Augustus, which meant grand.

In England and Western Europe, the use of family names came about gradually, between the eleventh and the sixteenth centuries. But certain groups took family names all at once, by decree. Jews in the Austrian empire were suddenly bidden to take names in 1787, and many of them chose poetic names, like Goldberg (golden mountain) or Blumenthal (valley of flowers). The Japanese did not all take surnames until commanded to do so by the Emperor Meiji in the nineteenth century.

As individuals began to mingle with strangers, their family ties became weaker. The use of a surname, however, was a constant reminder of their family duties, at least to one side of the family. The individual's loyalty was not necessarily to living relatives, but to a name, which had to be kept unsmirched through every difficulty.

Today in England and France, one cannot change his surname without court action. In America it isn't necessary to go to court to change a name, although some people find it more convenient. In general, surnames have lost the importance they had in past centuries. Although many old families still have a feeling of responsibility to their names, most of us have transferred this feeling to our country and our church. We use names freely, and often we use only first names, which show no family connections. This is another sign of our modern lifeway, in which the individual stands by himself, receiving almost as much help from strangers as he does from his family.

CHAPTER II

Childhood

Do you feel that eating worms or insects is disgusting and that you would choke if you tried to get them down? If you are female do you enjoy wearing a necklace and earrings, and if you are male would you tear them off in scorn? If you are a girl do you kiss your father, and if you are a boy would both you and he shy away from such a thing? The answer to all of these questions is probably yes, and most of the people in the United States would give the same reply. But why? That question is harder.

If you, an American, had been transported immediately after birth to live among the Australian natives, you would now be eating wormlike grubs and liking them. There they are eaten regularly at times of the year when other meat is scarce. If you had been taken to certain primitive tribes, you would feel men should, of course, wear necklaces at dances, while women should wear no ornaments at all. And if you had been born among your own European ancestors some hundreds of years ago, you would have thought it perfectly natural for a son to kiss his father. Among some Europeans, it is still the usual greeting.

These kinds of behavior, then, are not born in us. They are learned, and so are the feelings that go with them. It is true that each baby is born with some tendencies which make him different from other babies. He may be inclined toward aggressiveness, gentleness, nervousness, gaiety, or a dozen other attitudes or combinations of them. But what he learns is the way in which these attitudes may be expressed. One little tribe in New Guinea is reported to make a habit of bad temper and quarreling. Anyone there who feels the least bit irritated will fly into a rage, while the really aggressive person seems in a rage most of the time. In the New Mexico pueblo of Zuñi, where peace is the ideal, even the aggressive person speaks softly. All these people have learned what kinds of behavior are acceptable in their world. And the family has been the teacher.

Throughout the history of the human race, babies have been raised by their families. They have been dependent on adults not only for food and care, but for guidance in the ways of human life. Would a baby learn anything at all if he were not surrounded by human beings whom he wanted to grasp, to see, and, later, to approach on his own little feet? The few reports we have of children who were left almost completely alone tell us that they did not talk at all and began walking, or perhaps only crawling, much later than most children do. The love and attention that a family gives its child is very important to his learning process. Children in the wrong kind of orphanage, where they get little personal attention, seem dull and stupid, but when they are placed in a family with loving foster parents and interested playmates, their ability to learn increases.

Loving care will usually make a child responsive to teaching, but what he learns differs in various parts of the world. Modern Americans have been brought up to tend their houses, wear clothing, save money, and plan their activities by the clock. These ways of behaving seem perfectly natural to us, and we are shocked when we meet people who do not take care of their houses, do not wear clothes, do not save money, and are never on time. "Why can't they learn?" we ask. For the answer, let us look at an Apache Indian camp of some generations ago.

The camp is a collection of bush-covered wickiups, easily put up and easily abandoned. They are used only for sleeping and storage, for life is in the open. Naturally the owners do not value them or give them much care beyond a little sweeping. The children wear almost no clothing, for this makes it easier for the parents to keep them clean. Of course, they know all about the body and its functions, and they talk of these as casually as they talk

about food. White people are sometimes shocked at what they regard as their "dirty" language.

The main meal of the day is generally cooked in the late afternoon, but on this day it will be cooked a little later. The men are still away, and there is no point in starting the meal when their return is so uncertain. The women are chatting happily, and the children are playing. No one is impatient about the delay, for their stomachs are not conditioned to eating at any particular time.

After a while, a man and his wife enter the camp. He is carrying a bow and arrow, while she follows behind him, bent almost double under a huge load of firewood. Everyone understands this arrangement. There might be enemies on the trail or game to be chased. The man needs his hands free for his weapons, and the woman is well content with her own safe job. The boys and girls who see this every day will always feel that men should walk ahead, while their wives follow behind, carrying the heavy loads. Even when there are no enemies and no game, they will walk this way, for there are many customs which are followed even when the original reasons for them do not exist. Our own ancestors held out their hands in greeting to show that they carried no weapons. Today we still shake hands, although the danger of an attack is no longer present.

Two other Apaches arrive at the camp. They have good news. Scouting among the rocks, they saw a man with two loaded donkeys. He had been separated from his caravan, and it was simple to ambush him and kill him. It is easy to understand why they use this method of attack.

These Apaches are a small band, at war with all the whites and the Indians around them. Their camp has often been looted and their women kidnaped. They do not have enough men for an open battle, so their only recourse is to pick off their enemies from ambush. They hope that this will frighten others and keep them away. The Apache child sees and hears of this kind of behavior day after day. Later, if he goes to a white man's school, he will simply not understand if he is asked to "put up his fists and fight like a man."

Nor will he understand why any property should be put away and saved. The two scouts have killed one of the captured donkeys, and they distribute the meat throughout the camp, naturally giving special parts to their parents-in-law. There will be no meat left for the next day, but by then someone else may bring in game. Or perhaps the whole camp will have to go without eating. There is rarely an overabundance of food, and even when there is, the Apaches have no convenient way of preserving it. Later on, if a white teacher tries to tell Apache children about putting money in a bank, his words will not make much sense to them. And there will be plenty of other things which simply won't have meaning for these children, although they seem to us the natural way to behave.

A hundred years ago the tribes of Borneo were as warlike as the Apaches. However, they did more hand-to-hand fighting, and their aim was to produce fierce and aggressive warriors. A father might force his young son to stab a live slave over and over, so that he would get used to the sight of flowing blood. Like the other warriors of his tribe, he did get used to it. Tenderhearted missionaries from another civilization were met only with a polite smile when they pleaded against this practice. So might a gourmet, used to eating raw oysters, smile at the ignoramus who could not swallow them.

A wealthy Chinese boy of the same era had a very different pattern of behavior. He would probably call the Apache boy and the Borneo boy barbarians, and would want nothing to do with fighting. Also he was used to money, to saving and bargaining. But what about the endless rigmaroles of politeness, with a hidden meaning behind every word, which he was used to? "Let's get down to business!" might be the modern person's comment. But this boy's family had always lived in dangerous political situations, where it could not afford to make enemies. The safest course was politeness and more politeness. Underneath it, though, one tried to guess the other man's purpose and jockey him into a position where he would be at a disadvantage.

There is no space to describe the endless variations of behavior imbibed through childhood experience. But it is enthralling to study the kinds of behavior that are natural to different groups, to trace them to family attitudes, and to try to understand the conditions that brought these attitudes about. Even with oneself, it is revealing to consider which of our ideas were reasoned out and which were simply absorbed, for better or for worse, from the family.

The methods by which a child is taught in his early years are almost as various as the things he learns. Still,

we can make a rough distinction between people without reading and writing, who learn primarily by doing, and people in more complex societies, who depend on organized schooling. North and South American Indians, and primitive peoples in Africa and the South Seas, are good examples of this first type of society. Modern youngsters might well envy the children of these groups, for the "don'ts" are very few. Old-time Apaches had no clothes to soil, no houses to keep clean, and almost nothing that was breakable. Usually, there was very little discipline, though sometimes tales of frightening monsters were used. Pueblo Indian mothers in our Southwest evade responsibility by having a man, costumed as an ogre, come to the

door and inquire for bad children. Of course, the mother
assures the creature that her children are not bad. At least,
they will not be bad in the future. As for moral instruction,
that is done around the evening fire. The tales of Coyote
or Fox or Rabbit, who got into trouble through wrong-
doing, are told so often that they are permanently fixed in
the child's mind.

Discipline usually becomes more severe as a society
grows more complex. Even the simplest house neces-
sitates more rules for children than a temporary hut
does. It is not by chance that child training in the civi-
lized world so often involves whipping and punishment.
The Pueblo Indian mother who is shocked at learning

this fact has no idea of all the dangers and the possibilities for mistakes that surround a modern child in the street and at home.

On the other hand, primitive children have no comics and no moving pictures, so their play is mostly an imitation of what their elders do. Among the Apaches, little boys hunt rats and lizards, and little girls play house—very often tending a live baby in the family instead of a doll.

In all of these groups, the children are with grown people, at least with the women, most of the time. They do not live in a separate child's world, and they slip gradually into the ways of the group with little temptation to do otherwise.

About the age of seven or so, the children put on clothes. At this time, say the Papago Indians, the child has become a person. He has ceased to be completely absorbed in himself and is looking about the world. He becomes aware of the various relationships within the group, and almost unconsciously begins learning how to behave toward its different members. This is the time when the sexes separate. Among the Plains Indians, the brother and sister who have played so intimately together will, perhaps, never be alone with each other again until they are grown up and married. In South Africa, the boys begin to eat with the men instead of eating at home with the mother, the sisters, and the younger children. In the South Seas, girls begin to hide their faces from possible future in-laws. The child learns these and countless other customs by seeing them practiced and then by doing them himself.

At work, too, the boys follow the men, and the girls the women, learning by imitation rather than by hearing the job analyzed and explained beforehand. One is reminded of the learning process of lion cubs; they master the complicated art of hunting by watching their parents and trying the attack over and over again. Usually there are only a few arts that have to be taught, and primitive parents use the method of praise rather than punishment to encourage their children to learn. The Plains Indian father gave a feast when his boy had killed his first buffalo calf. The father or mother on the North Pacific coast did the same when the boy caught his first fish or the girl picked her first basket of berries.

In preliterate societies and in most literate ones as well, childhood was divided into two stages. The first was from birth to the age of outside contacts, and the second was from that time to young adulthood. As the children got older, their instructors were no longer merely the core family. Although they had no contact with strangers in the way modern children do, boys and girls of the Plains Indians and among groups in the South Seas might choose to leave home and visit with relatives for weeks at a time. For example, a boy in a mother-descent group who was the heir of his mother's brother might go to that uncle to be trained and, later, marry his daughter. Sometimes children learned from their contemporaries, or from other adults within the tribe. Where there were men's societies, boys might start their own clubhouse, or they might begin to frequent the men's clubhouse. This opened up a whole new area of experience. Little Moslem and East Indian children stayed with their mothers in seclusion until the age of outside contacts. Then the boys emerged to live with the men and learn from them, while the girls remained behind. In Europe during the Middle Ages, the father, occupied with war and politics, scarcely saw his small son until the child was ready to be trained in horsemanship and the use of arms.

From all indications, the human race still prefers to learn by doing. Textbooks and theoretical explanations are comparatively new things in our long history, and only a few people seem to take to them with real eagerness. But organized schooling, the bugbear of many a modern child, is the natural accompaniment of advanced technology. Even though this kind of learning sometimes includes no more than the three R's and a special craft or two, it takes a long time, for many of these things cannot be learned simply by doing them. Unlike the Indian boy, who learns to hunt by shooting an arrow, the modern boy must master many preliminaries before he can perform. This means sitting over a book or listening to long explanations.

In these complex societies, the family members have no time to do such teaching every day. Nor are they equipped to teach all the different professions. The result is education by a tutor or a schoolteacher, strangers from whom the child does not learn automatically, as he does when he absorbs his knowledge from the family. We shall not even begin to list the varieties of educational techniques, which include everything from learning the Koran by heart and reciting it in unison to individual research and

reports by pupils. The important point is this—as there are more subjects to learn and as the goals of education become more complicated, learning, after the early years, comes less from the family and more from teachers and schoolmates. This entails discipline, which may make school anything but loved, but on the other hand, it opens up a great variety of interests. A modern child has numerous careers to choose from, while the young Apache, for all his contentment, had only two or three.

Despite later influences of one kind or another, the child's early years within his family are likely to give his personality its deepest coloring. We used to consider such coloring an inborn characteristic of race, but studies have shown us now that habits of thought and action are acquired in the very early years, along with convictions about what is beautiful and ugly, right and wrong, and even which version of religion is the truest. Families differ greatly, of course; but within one nation, tribe, or social set, there is a general pattern of beliefs and behavior which they follow.

As we have seen, this pattern is by no means a matter of chance or whim. It originates from the life conditions of the group, and often continues to exist long after these conditions have changed. Each people did the best it could with the resources and the knowledge it had at hand, and slowly built up a system of beliefs and behavior to fit them. Such a system is called a culture, and study will show that each group and subgroup and sub-subgroup has its own. Culture includes all the characteristic features of a society at a given time, and it changes very slowly. Even a revolution can not wholly alter it. Its continuance depends chiefly on the family, which forms the child's world long before the influence of school, government, or any other institution is felt.

CHAPTER 12

Adolescence

"WHEN YOU were about sixteen," I asked an old Indian woman, "did you begin to think that your parents were stupid and bossy and you'd like to get away from them?"

"Get away? But I *was* away. I was married."

"Well, then, at fourteen. You were changing and growing then. Didn't you want to get out and do things?"

She smiled in memory. "Oh, yes. And I *was* doing things. I had just had my maiden's ceremony, and there was much to learn. I was a woman, and I wanted to be a good one."

I was startled by her answers, for I had supposed that all teen-agers experienced feelings of restlessness and a wish to break away from their families. "What about the boys of fourteen?" I asked. "Weren't they pretty wild?"

She shook her head. "Why should they have been wild? They had just become men, and they wanted to be treated as such. They worked very hard. And in the days when there was war, a boy would follow the war party and cook, carry burdens, and tend the horses. He was not a child."

This picture of the teen-ager was so different from my own that I wondered which of us was seeing the world askew. But when I began to study the many ways in which societies have attempted to handle the problems of adolescence, I realized that the restlessness and confusion of modern teen-agers are not at all characteristic of young people in other parts of the world and at other times in history.

These feelings exist in complex societies, because teen-agers are caught between the wish to go out in the world and be independent and the need for parental care and support. Nature—to use a short term for all the complicated life processes—brings about great physical changes in boys and girls during these years. Adults today sometimes pay no attention to these changes, and then the young folks are likely to whisper about them among themselves. Male voices deepen, hands and feet grow larger, and by their early teens most boys and girls are physically able to have families of their own. But our modern society rarely allows them to take on full adult responsibilities until much later. They need more training today than that which was needed to track an enemy or shoot an arrow.

During these years of training young people live with their parents and are supported by them. How should they be treated during this time? Should they be regarded as adults, as they were when girls were married at twelve and boys took swords and went to war at fifteen? The answer is usually no. Parents feel that a person who is being supported should also be obedient, and teachers feel that a youngster in the ninth grade, even if he is earning money, is not yet ready for the adult world. Who cannot see their point of view? But the result is that boys and girls must make their way slowly from childhood to adulthood, spending many restless years as half children, half adults.

Other societies have been able to handle this problem in a different way. By ordeals, initiations, and ceremonies, they have officially made their young people men and women, with entirely new jobs and privileges.

How would a modern American boy feel if, at the age of fourteen, he were placed naked on a hill of biting ants? That was the doorway into adult life for a Guiana Indian of the South American forest. If a boy stood the ordeal well, he could go out with the hunters and would soon be given a bride. Among the black Arunta of Australia, a boy went through two painful operations, performed with a stone knife and no anesthetic. The cutting was done with great ceremony, and all women were kept away on pain of death. It was a frightening experience, but the reward was magnificent. When the second operation was over, the boy was told religious secrets that were known only to men. This instruction came, not from his father but from the important old men of the group, who took him into their company and made him a potential equal. His final acceptance as one of them depended on his own manly achievements.

This initiation of boys into the tribe or clan was a well-known custom among primitive peoples. In Africa the youngsters might be taken into the bush for several months. There, under the supervision of a group of older men, they were put through a course of sprouts. This entailed short rations, teasing, and frightening, but also practice in hunting and instruction in the lore of the tribe. When Thonga boys in South Africa went through this process, the women were told that they had been swallowed by a monster, who would spit them up again only if they were brave and worthy. Once in a while, a boy really died under the treatment. Those who survived came back triumphant, covered by a cone of intermingled leaves and branches, with only their bare legs showing. Uttering strange cries, they walked through the village like something nonhuman. They were allowed a little time to run wild, steal food, and frighten the women; and then they began the work of men.

In Africa, in South America, and in the islands of the South Pacific, there were initiations of this general sort. Sometimes they involved a serious ordeal, like circumcision, flogging, scarring the body, knocking out some front teeth, or filing them into points. The very severity of the ordeal pointed up the value of the boy's new status. During it he wore costumes and masks, and was permitted to handle mysterious objects hitherto forbidden. This gave him a sense of importance and set him apart from all the

females, who were not allowed to touch these objects.

These initiations happened just at the time when a boy was feeling new strength, a new sense of adventure, and when nothing seemed too hard for him if it was exciting and active. But initiations did more than simply dispose of surplus energy. They were tests of a boy's skill and endurance and an opportunity for the older men to give instruction under very impressive circumstances. The boy who emerged was no longer considered a child. He was definitely a young man. True, if he now went out with the warriors or the hunters, he took the lowest place, was still subject to instruction, and probably had to do all the dirty work of the war expedition. But he was thoroughly proud of his new status, just as a freshman might be proud to do the will of important seniors in college.

In East Africa the Masai, a famous warlike tribe, circumcised boys between the ages of fourteen and sixteen. Then they went into barracks, where they stayed until about the age of twenty-five and acted as the defensive army of the country. They wore special elaborate costumes, with ostrich feathers on their heads, and they were fed on beef blood and milk. They were not expected to marry, although the girls of one age group were allowed to visit them and dance. When their service drew to an end, a new group of boys who had been circumcised were expected to drive the former group out and occupy the barracks. Sometimes it might take a year or so of strife before they succeeded. Then the first group of warriors left the barracks, married, and set up as important citizens and cattle owners.

Another form of entry into grown-up life was joining the men in their clubhouse. A good many groups had a special house where the men spent almost all their time and sometimes even slept. It was used for craft work, for work on ceremonial objects which women must not see, and for gossip and discussion. There were such houses in Melanesia, Alaska, and here and there among other groups. At about the age of seven, that important age when children put on clothing and began to do more of the work of adults, a boy might join his father and perhaps sit in the very lowest and least comfortable place in the men's house, working up gradually as he grew older. In the South Pacific, a Banks Island boy joined the lowest "oven" in the club. From there he could buy his way up by giving feasts.

The fighting Indians of the plains also had societies, with emblems, songs, and sometimes vows of suicidal bravery. Among the Mandan and Hidatsa there were ten societies, arranged in an ascending order of importance. The lowest was the Stone Hammers, for boys of ten or eleven, and the highest was the Ravens, for retired old men. The Stone Hammers organized themselves and bought out the group higher up, the Lumpwoods, by giving them a feast. The Lumpwoods then bought out the next group, and so on. At some points there might be delay and argument, and the whole process would be held up. Other tribes might have only a few societies, with no age requirements, but they always had to do with war and service to the tribe.

There were a number of other ways, more or less

arduous, through which a boy graduated from childhood into manhood. The Pueblo villages of our Southwest were little religious states, and the public officials also had priestly duties. Every boy at maturity was initiated into the ceremonial life of his people, but without the long ordeal of a bush school. When a Zuñi boy put on the

kachina mask, which he was entitled to wear at a certain age, he was, for a time, actually regarded as a rain-bringing spirit.

North American Indians had no circumcision and little that resembled a bush school. There were no physical operations at the entry into adulthood, except for an occasional tattooing. Instead, at least for boys, this period was regarded as a time of profound spiritual experience, which each boy must achieve for himself. One way of achieving this was by seeing a vision. The "vision quest" was especially customary of hunting tribes, all the way across the United States. A hunting life is so full of uncertainties that skill and endurance alone cannot assure success. It is also necessary to have luck, and the Indians believed that luck came from the spirits. In late childhood, youth, or early manhood, according to the area, the hunter or warrior went into the wilds to starve and thirst, perhaps to torture himself, in the hope that some spirit would take pity on him and give him this incalculable power.

After days of starvation, a vision usually came, as it did to monks in the Middle Ages. An animal or plant, perhaps the wind or a cloud, came in human form and spoke to the dreamer. It taught him a song and gave him a token, and these assured him of the desired luck in hunting, racing, war, even in medicine. This did not mean that the dreamer could trust in his luck with no further effort. He worked with a will to grow even more skillful and hardened, but he worked with a conviction of success. Indian boys who failed to have visions felt uninspired and helpless.

Sometimes visions were induced by a careful dose of the dream-bringing plant Datura, or Jimson weed, after which the boy was given a lecture, bidding him always to share food and respect the old. But generally vision experiences had nothing to do with instruction. American Indian boys were prepared for marriage and other adult responsibilities at another time, by the older men of the tribe.

Some tribes had no ceremonies for boys at all, and it is

always interesting to try to understand why this happened and what sort of education was given instead.

In every society there were fewer ordeals for girls, since they already had the ordeal of childbirth before them. But in Africa, where the bush school for boys and the physical operation were so important, many groups felt that something of that sort should be done for girls. The Kikuyu performed an operation on them to make marriage and childbearing easier. Both girls and boys went to bush schools and marched in parade on the same day to receive the blessings of the elders. Chaga girls were taught about the human body, the teacher illustrating with marks on sticks. They also learned how to care for a husband and children. Some tribes scarred their girls' backs or pierced their ears as an aid to beauty and a sign that they were ready for marriage.

The most usual treatment for girls was to keep them in seclusion for a while, after the great event of maidenhood had occurred. We have spoken of the awe that many primitive people felt toward childbirth, and the custom of keeping a woman away from other people, especially men, while she was under this strong spirit influence. Girls, when they first attained the power of childbearing, were felt to be under this same influence and were treated in the same way. At that time, and often at every monthly period afterward, some tribes placed a girl in a special hut and gave her special foods. Some African girls stayed in the hut for months, until they were fat and pale—a great sign of beauty.

This shutting away of the girl at maidenhood was

probably a very ancient custom, practiced long before there were any bush schools or vision quests. Some tribes had a special hut outside the village, or perhaps various families had huts, in which women or girls under this supernatural influence might retire. In South America, the girl often lay in a hammock, perhaps near the ceiling, where the smoke of the fire, thought to have healing properties, could surround her.

On the Pacific coast, where Indians lived in huge wooden houses, there was a small compartment at one end of the house where the girl undergoing her maidenhood seclusion could stay. Here she might remain six months or more, eating special foods and receiving instruction from the older women, not only in the duties of matrimony but also in crafts. She wasn't completely cut off from the outside world however. The huge boards which formed the walls of her house were attached to the uprights by slings of vines instead of nails, and they could be raised like the slats of a Venetian blind. There are stories about suitors who stood outside the house, raised the board, and whispered love songs to the secluded maiden. Sometimes a hand, bearing a gift, could reach inside. This might be pleasant for the girl but, as we have seen, nothing could come of it unless a suitor was able to pay the proper bride price to the girl's father.

Some Indians of southern California had a very elaborate ceremony for girls. They had to lie on a bed of hot sand—supposed to be very medicinal—for several days, while the women of the group gathered around to sing songs of marriage for them. Other tribes in that area drew

a picture, representing the world, upon the sand. The girl spit a ball of tobacco into it, thus making herself a part of the world. She was then shown figures, frightening creatures, and told, "See, these are alive. These will think well of you if you believe. If you do not believe, they are going to kill you. You must not be heedless, a dissembler, or stingy. You must not look sideways or receive a person in your house with anger. It is not proper. Think well of your elder relatives, and welcome your daughters-in-law and your brothers-in-law when they arrive at your house."

Instruction like this, given in public after a very elaborate ceremony, was, of course, most impressive. For both boys and girls, reaching the age when they were no longer children was an important public event. Everything was done to make them feel that they now had new responsibilities and, also, that they were respected. Quite often the parents had a new social status because they had had a child initiated. The whole arrangement was an excellent way of installing young people in their new place in society and giving them a sense of honor and responsibility.

In more complex societies there were no ordeals at this coming-of-age period and no bush schools. Generally, there was no ceremony for girls at all, but there was a celebration when a boy reached the age of manhood. A Roman boy made a sacrifice to the household gods, and then took off his childhood costume and hung it up. After that there was a grand procession to the forum with his father and all his father's adherents, where his name was inscribed in the roll of citizens. Finally, there was a great feast at his father's home. In the Middle Ages, a Moslem boy who had finished his study of the Koran preached a sermon, and his achievement was celebrated with a feast. The high-caste boy in India celebrated his coming of age by putting on a cord, which was worn across his chest from the right shoulder to the left hip.

Our modern life has no special way of marking the end of childhood and the beginning of adult responsibilities. At a certain age, children change from elementary school to high school, or they may be confirmed or admitted to membership in a church. But vows like those of the Kikuyu children, who promise to feel responsibility to the tribe and to act like adults in all things, are lacking in our life. Perhaps it would be well if we could find an equivalent of this custom for teen-agers today, and also some honorable and important work to occupy their energy.

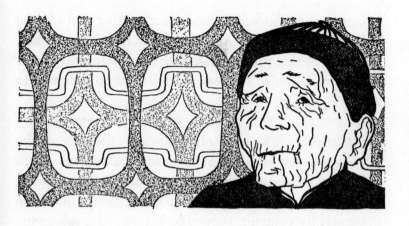

CHAPTER 13

Old Age

"PLENTY GRAY hairs!" said the old Indian to the young white official, whose hair was solid brown. It was a high compliment, for in the thinking of the Indian's people, the older a man was, the more he would know and the more wisely he would act. This was the attitude of a large number of primitive groups, and we can understand why. In societies where the store of knowledge was limited, one man, in the course of a lifetime, could master most of it.

In many groups a man put on a different costume, took a different name, and assumed a new social position when he passed middle age. An Iroquois who had given up war no longer wore the scalp lock, but let his hair grow long.

A Comanche who had turned from fighting and raiding began giving feasts. In Africa a Kipsigi held a beer-drinking feast at this time of life, and the ceremonial leader sanctified a wooden stool on which he was now allowed to sit.

In general, a man's power and influence increased in his later years. The head of the society, the clan, or the family unit was usually its oldest man, unless he was in his dotage. He often held lesser positions first, and gradually worked up to his high rank. Among groups that were governed by councils, only elderly men, as a rule, were members. If young men attended, they were expected to listen without speaking. This arrangement worked well where conditions remained fairly stable over a long period of time or where the oldest man could apply what he knew to current affairs. It did not work as well in times of violent change, when young men, eager for new ways and full of new ideas, might have been helpful. Today, incidentally, the All-Pueblo Council of our Southwest is purposely bringing in young men and listening to them.

Even if an old man had no official position, he often played an important role in the group. In the days when there were no books, his memory provided information, and people came to him for help of one kind or another. At American Indian ceremonies one constantly hears people say, "This must be done by some old man who knows the songs," or, "We must ask an old man to show us the method of body painting." Often he was paid for this service. If he had had a successful life, he might be asked to be a godfather or to instruct a boy at the time of initiation. When a Plains Indian boy had killed his first buffalo calf, his father would give a feast for the prominent old men of the tribe, who would praise the boy and encourage him to further endeavor.

Many early societies based their class divisions on age, rather than on wealth or rank. The ancient Peruvians and other peoples divided life into a series of periods, from childhood up to extreme old age. Many at least separated the young, who were the learners; the adults, who were the warriors and childbearers; and the elders, who were the teachers and councilors.

In our society, most of the teachers are young women. It is true that their vitality and their knowledge of new methods give brightness to the lessons. On the other hand, their students miss something that primitive children had —sharing the wisdom and experience of the important members of the tribe and being approved and encouraged by them. No one was rude to the teacher when he was an old man, full of magic lore. He was looked up to, and his good opinion was eagerly sought after. And the old man felt that helping all the younger people was an important responsibility. It is well to remember, also, that old men are capable of new ideas. Judging a person's capacities on age alone may be no more valid in this age of the young than it was in the days when a man was considered wise just because he was old.

Old women did not have official positions except in mother-descent groups, where they could be ceremonial leaders or the heads of women's societies. In most tribes, however, they were the teachers and godparents of young girls, just as men were of boys. Even among father-descent groups, the wife of the old male leader sometimes led the women on food-gathering parties or in gardening activities. And in some West African kingdoms the king's mother was almost as important as the ruler.

Women past childbearing age sometimes had privileges never allowed them in youth. Since they were no longer imbued with the mysterious birth magic, men did not fear them. Some American Indian women had visions and became healers, although they couldn't attain the eminence of men. They could dance and perform in public now, which maidens were not permitted to do. While southern California girls were baking on their hot sand beds, or while girls on the Pacific coast were secluded in their cubicles, old women came and sang marriage songs of their own invention. When Papago warriors returned from battle, old women grabbed the scalps they brought and danced madly with them.

Even very old people who were past their usefulness received consideration in most places. Not only their families but the whole group took care of them. This care was a kind of pension, a reward for past services. In the South Seas, where there were many food taboos, especially for women, these were all removed in old age. The Arapesh in New Guinea and the Arunta in Australia saved the choicest tidbits for the old. Among the Mandan and other Plains Indians, a young man gained special acclaim by giving feasts for the old or presenting them with horses from his raids.

But there was another side to this picture. Among

wandering people, where food was scarce, it was impossible to give tidbits to the old or, sometimes, to feed them at all. It was no kindness to drag feeble, rheumatic people over Arctic snows or barren deserts. Therefore, the old sometimes preferred to be left behind to die quickly. This custom was followed by the central Eskimos, the Paiute Indians of Nevada, and the Aymara of Lake Titicaca in the Andes. A Koryak father in Siberia might even ask his son to put a rope around his neck, so that he could die quickly. If the son refused to do this, the old man might have a slow, painful death, and he would feel ill treated.

All peoples believed that the souls of the dead had some kind of afterlife, although it was usually not eternal. It might endure until all who had known the dead person in this life were also gone or until he was reincarnated in a child or an animal. The home of the dead was rarely thought of as a pleasant place, but it was not a hell either. It was a dim abode which the ghost was anxious to leave, and it was important that the living make him content to stay there. So gifts and supplies were buried or burned with the dead, and sometimes sacrifices were made afterward.

There were two very different attitudes toward the dead. One meant remembering the dead and regarding them almost as gods. In fact, the only worship practiced by some African tribes was worship of ancestral spirits, whose shrines stood in every kraal. Many groups in southeast Asia and the South Pacific also worshiped ancestors. On one Melanesian island the ghost of the latest dead family member was believed to watch every act of his

descendants and to punish them with sickness or bad luck if they misbehaved.

It was in China that ancestor worship became most famous. Tablets, representing the dead of the last five generations, were set up in the family's main hall. It was believed that they could answer questions by allowing objects thrown in front of them to fall in ways that meant yes or no. The tablets were regarded as older family members who had to be honored and cared for. Food was served them regularly until they were thought to be established in the next world. Then, periodically, they were offered gifts of imitation clothing and money. Family members saluted them on every important occasion, so that they could share in all the activities of the household. For such ceremonies, a son was essential, for a daughter served the tablets of her husband. So, in old China, the need for sons was not only practical and emotional, but also religious.

The other attitude toward the dead, and one that was especially common among the American Indians, was fear. Not fear of the departed person himself, but fear that, in his loneliness, he would want to take some relative to the land of the dead for company. We have noted how this fear caused people to avoid the use of his name or any words like it. Many people also burned down his house or at least deserted it for a time. For days the family let themselves go in violent grief—weeping, slashing off their hair, and gashing themselves. Those who had handled the corpse went through a long purification, somewhat like that of women after childbirth. When all had been done, they settled down to a new life, with the dead excluded. They turned again to their homes, their work, their children; and family life went on.

The families described in this book lived under conditions very different from those of modern America. Their ways of life grew out of these conditions, and lasted long after they had changed. If many of these customs seem strange, even fantastic to us today, it is because we do not understand the reasons for them or how they really worked.

Every early family had the same basic needs. In the first place, the very first place, it had to be strong. This

meant increasing its numbers by having many children
and by forming alliances through marriage. In the second
place, it needed unity. It could remain strong only if every
member put the interests of the family first. Sometimes
the father was the head of the family; sometimes the
mother or her brother was. But whatever the system of
rule, the family was always united. Its members spent
their time together, sharing knowledge and work, food
and shelter, danger and pleasure.

Modern conditions are such that families need no
longer live and act together as they once had to do. Our
lifeway has forced us to live much of the time as individuals. Even those who admire the old unity cannot achieve
it today. But it is possible to study the customs of the old
family organization and decide what its real virtues were.
Then we can try to find new methods of gaining the bene-
fits of this earlier way of life. If there was good in such
things as loyalty, practical education, friendship between
the old and the young, how can the same good be brought
about today, using other people and other institutions in
place of the family?

Biographical Note

RUTH M. UNDERHILL was born in Ossining, N. Y. She attended the Ossining School for Girls and was graduated from Vassar College. After studying at the London School of Economics, she worked for the Massachusetts Society for the Prevention of Cruelty to Children, for the New York Charity Organization Society, and for the American Red Cross in Italy, in charge of Italian orphanages. She received her Ph. D. from Columbia University, and during the time she was there she was an assistant in anthropology at Barnard College. She was granted fellowships by Columbia University to do field work among the Papago and Mohave Indians of Arizona. Dr. Underhill worked as an anthropologist for the United States Department of Agriculture from 1936

to 1937 and had the title of Supervisor of Indian Education
for the United States Bureau of Indian Affairs from 1937 to
1949. During those years she traveled and lived on Indian
reservations. From 1947 to 1952 she was Professor of Anthropology at Denver University and is now Professor Emeritus.

Dr. Underhill has recently made a series of ten tape-re-
corded programs, interviewing Navajo, Pueblo, and Sioux
Indians. She is now giving a series of thirty lectures about
United States Indians for National Educational Television.
These programs are being kinescoped for use by educational
institutions all over the country. She also works with Indians
in Denver, helping them to adjust to living off the reservation.

Among Dr. Underhill's publications are five books about
the Papago Indians, published by Columbia University
Press, University of California Press, the American Anthropological Association, the University of New Mexico Press,
and the Indian Bureau. She has also written, for the Indian
Bureau, books about the Pueblo, California, and Pacific
Northwest Indians, and many pamphlets. Her most recent
books are *Red Man's America*, published in 1953 by The University of Chicago Press, and *The Navajos*, published in 1956
by University of Oklahoma Press.

For most of her life Dr. Underhill has been an avid
mountain climber and has enjoyed canoeing and skiing. Now
travel and gardening are her chief hobbies.

Dr. Underhill's interests have taken her to many parts of
the world. For example, she has lived on a co-operative farm
in Israel, with a family in India, and in native villages both
in Australia and in New Zealand. She has also lived for
several months at a time in England, Italy, Spain, and
Germany, and has traveled through the entire subcontinent
of India. Recently she took a trip around the world. She

has given papers at international anthropological conventions in England, Austria, and Brazil. In the United States she has lived in Ossining, Sante Fe, and Washington, D. C. Her present home is in Denver, Colorado.

Dr. Underhill is a member of the American Anthropological Association, the American Folklore Society, and the New Mexico Historical Society. She is a fellow of the American Association for the Advancement of Science. To be qualified for this honor, a person must have a Ph. D. and be actively engaged in work in his special field.

First Came the Family is Dr. Underhill's first book for young people.

Index

Indicates illustrations

Adolescence. *See* Teen-agers

Africans, 37, 38, 47, 77, 96, 104, 106, 112-114, 121, 127, 128, 129, 130, 132, 136, 140, 143, 150, 157, 163-164, 176, 178, 188, 189*, 195, 204, 207
  See also individual tribes

Alaskans, 192

Aleuts, 129

Amazons, 112-113

American Indians, 30, 38, 41*, 47, 50, 54-55, 60, 62, 63*, 66-67, 70, 96, 135, 138*, 141-142, 144, 145*, 150-151, 157-158, 161, 162, 165, 176, 180, 185-186, 193-195, 201, 202, 204, 209
  See also South American Indians and individual tribes

Americans, 22-24, 39, 41, 73, 107, 118, 122, 131, 155, 161, 167, 168, 170, 181*

Ancestor worship, 207-209, 208*

Andaman Islanders, 25

Anglo-Saxons, 38, 56-58, 67, 78, 104-105, 106, 107, 163, 165, 166, 167

Apache Indians, 124, 139, 170-174, 171*, 175, 176, 178, 183

Arabs, 30, 60, 65, 114-117, 149

Arunta, 61, 187, 204

Asians, 38, 96, 106, 114, 207
    See also individual countries

Australian tribes, 50, 71, 120, 127, 129, 144, 152, 168-169
    See also Arunta

Avoidance, 123-127, 125*

Aymara, 207

Basques, 143

Bemba, 84-85, 138

Borneans, 161, 174-175

Bride price, 56, 75*-83, 79*, 92, 106-107, 111, 113, 118, 132, 135

Brother marriage, 135-136

Burmese, 96, 139

Bush schools, 188, 193, 195

California Indians, 142-143, 148, 196-199, 204

Castes, 57, 65-66

Chagas, 195

Chickasaw Indians, 91

Childbearing, 138-147, 143*
    attitudes toward, 138-139, 140, 141, 155
    charms and prayers for, 139
    seclusion of women, 140-143, 142*

Child marriage, 71-72

Children
    attitudes toward, 151-155
    care of, 18, 21, 25-26, 150-155, 153*, 168*, 169-170

death of, 139-140, 147-149
discipline of, 176*-178, 177*
education of, 51, 168-184, 181*, 202-203
naming of, 157-158, 159*
Chinese, 38-39, 53-54, 57, 61, 67, 68*-69*, 96, 97, 98*, 99*, 117-118, 136, 139, 162, 175, 208-209
Clans, 38-40, 51, 53-54, 56-58, 61-62, 63*, 85-86
Clubhouses, 128, 129-130, 152, 192
Comanche Indians, 202
Coming-of-age ceremonies, 139, 185*, 187, 189*, 193*
bush schools, 188, 193, 195
celebrations, 199-200
clubhouses and societies, 192
costumes and masks, 188-191, 193
instruction, 187-188, 194, 195, 196-199
operations, 187, 191, 195
ordeals, 187, 188
seclusion of girls, 195-196, 197*
vision quests, 194
Common-law marriage, 104-105
Concubines, 111, 114-118, 115*
Core family, 22-26, 27, 29-30, 34, 51, 161
Cradleboard, 138*, 150-151
Creek Indians, 39, 52, 91, 112, 135, 136, 164*
Cross-cousin, 48*
Crow Indians, 38, 47-48, 50, 91
Culture, 183-184

Death
attitudes toward, 207-209
of child, 139-140, 147-149
of mate, 132-137
of old people, 204-207, 205*
Divorce, 131-132, 133*, 139

Dower, 82
Dowry, 82-83, 92-93

East Indians, 39, 57, 65-66, 70, 71-72, 83, 96, 97-100, 114,
    136, 138, 163, 179-180, 200
Education, 51, 168-184, 181*, 202-203
Egyptians, 65, 114
Elopement, 82
Endogamy, 62-66
English. See Anglo-Saxons
Eskimos, 25, 119-120*, 121*, 140, 148, 152-155, 205*, 207
Exogamy, 27, 61-65, 73

Family functions, 41-58, 43*, 168-184
    economic help, 56
    education, 51, 168-184, 181*
    police duty, 51-57
    social life, 42-51
Father descent. See Patrilineal system
Fox Indians, 39, 55-56
French, 106, 167

Greeks, 38, 83, 128, 148-149

Haida Indians, 157, 159*
Harems, 114-117, 115*
Hawaiians, 65
Hebrews. See Jews
Hidatsa Indians, 127
Hopi Indians, 37, 39, 82, 93-94, 112, 128, 129

Idaho Indians, 151, 152
Incas, 65
Indians, American. See American Indians
Indians, East. See East Indians

Initiations. *See* Coming-of-age ceremonies
Iroquois Indians, 33, 37, 38, 39, 81-82, 112, 135, 158, 201

Japanese, 86-87, 136, 166
Jews, 89, 130-131, 135, 144, 150, 163, 166

Kikuyu, 195, 200
Kipsigis, 61, 202
Kirghiz, 124

Love and romance, 69-70, 72-74, 86-87
Lovedu, 45, 77

Madagascans, 140
Makah Indians, 83-84, 92-93
Mandan Indians, 192, 204
Manus tribe, 78, 96, 124
Marriage, 26-27, 29, 38, 42-45, 57
  civil and religious, 90, 100, 103-107
  common-law, 104-105
  infidelity, 52, 53-54
  See also Marriage considerations and Married life
Marriage broker, 67, 69*
Marriage considerations, 60-69
  character of mate, 68-69
  family advantages, 66-67
  family relationships, 60-66
Marriage counselors, 74
Married life, 122-137
  avoidance, 123-127, 125*
  death of mate, 132-137
  division of work, 33-37, 109-110, 128-131
  divorce, 131-132, 133*, 139
  separation of sexes, 128
Masai, 73, 191

Mates, multiple, 109*-121
  concubines, 111, 114-118, 115*
  harems, 114-117, 115*
  monogamy, 118, 120-121
  monogyny, 112
  polyandry, 118-119
  polygamy, 109*, 115*, 120, 121
  polygyny, 109*-118, 115*, 121, 132-135, 136
  reasons for, 109-112, 117, 118, 119, 120-121
  wife lending, 119-120*, 121*
Mates, winning of, 75-87
  bride price, 56, 75*-83, 79*, 92, 106-107, 111, 113, 118,
    132, 135
  capture, 85-86
  dower, 82
  dowry, 82-83, 92-93
  elopement, 82
  tests, 68, 83-85, 84*, 92
Matrilineal system, 33, 34, 85*, 37, 127, 129-130, 132, 135,
  179, 203
Matrilocal, 34, 81-82, 112, 124-127
Maya Indians, 151
Melanesians, 47, 49, 128, 164, 192, 207
Mohammedans, 82, 100, 114, 128, 144, 157, 163, 179-180,
  199-200
  See also individual countries
Monogamy, 118, 120-121
Monogyny, 112
Mormons, 118
Mother descent. *See* Matrilineal system

Names, 156-167
  change of, 164*-165, 167
  history of, 163-167
  naming of children, 157-158, 159*

nicknames, 162, 165
praise names, 163-164
use of, 156-157, 158-163
Navaho Indians, 37, 39, 51, 55, 61, 91-92, 112, 125*, 127, 132, 133*
New Guinea tribes, 169, 204

Old people, 201*-210
attitudes toward, 201
care of, 204
change in status of, 201-202
death of, 204-207, 205*
in education, 202-203
in government, 202
privileges of, 204
Omaha Indians, 39, 109-110, 144-147, 158

Pacific coast Indians, 37, 47, 92-93, 148, 162, 179, 196, 204
Pacific Islanders. *See* South Pacific tribes
Paiute Indians, 25, 26, 207
Papago Indians, 27-29, 28*, 45-46, 59, 69, 90-91, 111, 138, 140-141, 178, 204
Parallel cousin, 49*
Parental care, 9-21, 25-26
birds, 13-16
fish, 9-11, 12, 13-14
human beings, 18, 21, 25-26, 150-155, 153*, 168*, 169-170
insects, 11-13*, 18-21
mammals, 16-18, 19*, 25
reptiles, 11
See also Children
Patrilineal system, 30, 31*, 33-34, 37, 45, 57-58, 77, 78, 118, 127, 132, 135
Patrilocal, 34, 37, 81

Persians, 114, 128
Peruvians, 203
Plains Indians, 37, 47, 48-49, 73, 78, 128, 130, 158, 164, 178, 179, 202-203, 204
Police duty, 51-57
Polyandry, 118-119
  definition of, 118
  reasons for, 118-119
Polygamy, 109*, 115*, 120-121
Polygyny, 109*-118, 115*, 121, 132-135, 136
  definition of, 110-111
  reasons for, 109-112
Praise names, 163-164
Pregnancy. See Childbearing
Pueblo Indians, 129, 176*-178, 177*, 193

Romans, 38, 57, 60, 83, 86, 100-103, 101*, 138, 166, 199

Samoans, 45
Scottish, 39, 104
Seclusion of women
  at maidenhood, 195-196, 197*
  during pregnancy, 140-143, 142*
  during wedding, 93, 96-97, 99*
Siberians, 30, 47, 78, 86, 123-124, 207
Sister marriage, 111-112
Social life, 42-51
South American Indians, 37, 47, 73, 91, 124, 129, 143*, 176, 187, 188, 196
South Pacific tribes, 34, 37, 50, 73, 78, 79*, 114, 124, 127, 129, 143, 152, 153*, 161, 176, 178, 179, 188, 192, 204, 207
South Sea tribes. See South Pacific tribes
Stem family, 29-30, 38

Teen-agers, 185-200
  problems of, 186-187, 200
  See also Coming-of-age ceremonies
Tibetans, 118-119
Toda tribe, 119
Turks, 100, 114

Weddings, 88-108, 101*
  clothing, 88-89, 92, 94, 95, 96, 97, 99, 103
  feasts, 89, 90, 91, 92, 94-95, 97, 100, 103, 105
  fertility symbols, 90, 92, 97, 103, 105
  processions, 88-89, 91, 94, 95, 96-97, 98*, 99*, 100, 103,
    105
  seclusion of bride, 93, 96-97, 99*
Widows, 135-137
Wife lending, 119-120*, 121*
Work, division of, 33-37, 109-110, 128-131

Yurok Indians, 78-81

Zulus, 30, 33, 38, 75*-76, 77, 94-96, 113, 122*, 123
Zuñi Indians, 34, 68, 112, 128, 129, 150, 169, 193